Scientometrics Recent Advances

Edited by Suad Kunosic and Enver Zerem

Published in London, United Kingdom

IntechOpen

Supporting open minds since 2005

Scientometrics Recent Advances
http://dx.doi.org/10.5772/intechopen.77450
Edited by Suad Kunosic and Enver Zerem

Contributors
Ligen Yu, Boxuan Yu, Bowei Yu, Fernando Juliani, Fabio Silva, Otavio Oliveira, Luis César Barbosa, Thaís Nunhes, Jorge Guimarães, Cristina Haeffner, Sonia Zanotto, Helena Nader, Denis Čeke, Suad Kunosic, Enver Zerem, Sadia Vancauwenbergh, Zhiyong Liu, Lei Ji

First published in London, United Kingdom, 2019 by IntechOpen
IntechOpen is the global imprint of INTECHOPEN LIMITED, registered in England and Wales, registration number: 11086078, 7th floor, 10 Lower Thames Street, London, EC3R 6AF, United Kingdom
Printed in Croatia

British Library Cataloguing-in-Publication Data
A catalogue record for this book is available from the British Library

Additional hard and PDF copies can be obtained from orders@intechopen.com

Scientometrics Recent Advances
Edited by Suad Kunosic and Enver Zerem
p. cm.
Print ISBN 978-1-78984-712-3
Online ISBN 978-1-78984-713-0
eBook (PDF) ISBN 978-1-78985-613-2

Meet the editors

Suad Kunosic is an associate professor in the Department of Physics, Faculty of Natural Sciences and Mathematics, University of Tuzla, Bosnia and Herzegovina. He obtained his PhD from the Faculty of Natural Sciences and Mathematics, University of Tuzla. He was Dean of Faculty of Natural Sciences and Mathematics, University of Tuzla from 2014 to 2016. Dr. Kunosic's research interests include biophysics, radiology, medical physics, scientometrics and scientific ranking. In April 2018, together with his colleague Dr. Zerem, Dr. Kunosic presented computer software that simply computes the Z-score (new science metrics system) as well as its components. He has published more than 20 scientific papers in referred journals (most of them in WoS (CC/SCI)) and he is co-author of one international book.

Dr. Enver Zerem is Professor of Internal Medicine at the University of Mostar in Mostar, Bosnia and Herzegovina. He received his medical degree from the University of Belgrade, Serbia, and PhD from the University of Tuzla, Bosnia. His research interests focus on the management of acute pancreatitis and application of interventional ultrasound in gastroenterology and hepatology. He is also interested in scientific publishing and science metrics systems and he has published several articles about both. Dr. Zerem has authored about 200 peer-reviewed articles, reviews and book chapters. He is a member of the Academy of Sciences and Arts of Bosnia and Herzegovina. He currently serves on the editorial boards and as a reviewer for several prestigious scientific journals.

Contents

Preface

In recent years, academic advancement and access to funds that stimulate scientific research have been conditioned by the scientific production of individual scientists, as well as the production of scientific centers, institutes and universities. This has led to an increase in interest in the accelerated assessment and ranking of scientists and scientific institutions. Scientometry is a sub-discipline of information sciences that measures achievement in science, the most significant of which is the number and value of publications of scientific research. While it is generally accepted that the impact factor (IF) and the total number of citations of all articles published in a scientific journal are the most relevant parameters of the importance of the journal, the significance of the scientific contribution of individual researchers is much more difficult to assess. This is because the value of their scientific production cannot be directly expressed in the importance of the journals in which their articles are published. At the same time, the ranking of scientific institutions, such as universities, institutes and other scientific centers, is done separately from ranking scientists and various additional criteria.

This book covers the following topics: data quality and ranking system, bibliometrics and its applications, scientific collaboration and citation analysis, and the future of scientometry. It provides the reader with a detailed insight into relevant scientometric methods and criteria, their individual strengths and weaknesses in the process of ranking scientists, scientific centers and institutions, as well as their application to the process of planning scientific projects and isolated medical specialties.

We want to express our sincere gratitude and appreciation to all the co-authors who have contributed their work to this book.

Suad Kunosic
Department of Physics,
Faculty of Natural Sciences and Mathematics,
University of Tuzla,
Bosnia and Herzegovina

Enver Zerem
Department of Medical Sciences,
Academy of Sciences and Arts of Bosnia and Herzegovina,
University Džemal Bijedić Mostar,
Bosnia and Herzegovina

Section 1

Data Quality and Ranking System

Chapter 1

Data Quality Management

Sadia Vancauwenbergh

Abstract

Data quality is crucial in measuring and analyzing science, technology and innovation adequately, which allows for the proper monitoring of research efficiency, productivity and even strategic decision making. In this chapter, the concept of data quality will be defined in terms of the different dimensions that together determine the quality of data. Next, methods will be discussed to measure these dimensions using objective and subjective methods. Specific attention will be paid to the management of data quality through the discussion of critical success factors in operational, managerial and governance processes including training that affect data quality. The chapter will be concluded with a section on data quality improvement, which examines data quality issues and provides roadmaps in order to improve and follow-up on data quality, in order to obtain data that can be used as a reliable source for quantitative and qualitative measurements of research.

Keywords: data quality, data quality measurement, data quality management, data quality improvement

1. Introduction

Over the past decades, research organizations, administrations and researchers have been collecting data that describe both the input as well as the output side of research. This has resulted in an enormous pile of data on publications, projects, patents, ... researchers and their organizations that are collected within database systems or current research information systems (CRIS). Such data systems are created according to specific goals and use purposes of individual organizations, which reflects their specific nature and the surrounding context in which they operate. However, over time these data systems, institutions as well as the research ecosystem at large have evolved, thereby potentially threatening the quality of the collected data and the resulting data analyses, particularly if no formal data quality management policy is being implemented. This chapter introduces the readers into the concept of data quality and provides methods to assess and improve data quality, in order to obtain data that can be used as a reliable source for quantitative and qualitative measurements of research.

2. Definition of data quality

In general, data can be considered of high quality if the data is fit to serve a purpose in a given context, for example, in operations, decision making and/or planning [1]. Although this definition of data quality seems to be straightforward, many other definitions exist that differ in terms of the qualitative or quantitative approach towards defining the concept of data quality.

2.1 Qualitative approach

In the qualitative approach, specific attention is drawn to defining data quality in terms of the different aspects, also termed dimensions. In 1996, Wang and Strong developed a data quality framework based on a two-stage survey on data quality aspects important to data consumers, and captured these dimensions in a hierarchical manner [2]. This model clusters 20 different data quality dimensions into four major categories: that is, intrinsic, contextual, representational and access data quality. Although the basis of this model still stands, some minor changes have been made over the years resulting in the model depicted in **Table 1** [3].

In brief, the *intrinsic* category comprises dimensions that define the accuracy of the data, that is, the extent to which data is certified, error-free, and reliable, as well as the objectivity of the data based on facts and impartial, and their reputation based on its sources or content. The *contextual* data quality category comprises dimensions that must be considered within the context of a specific objective for which one holds the data, that is, the data should be relevant, up to date, of an appropriate amount, yet complete, and ready for use for the stated objective. The *representational* category contains dimensions that reflect how the data are presented within a data system. Dimensions concerning the format of the data, that is, concise and consistent representation, as well as their compatibility, their interpretability and whether they are easy to understand, are considered. The last category is focused on the *accessibility* category that also defines aspects of data quality. Although this category is not always considered in the literature [4], this is an important aspect of overall data quality. The related dimensions include the accessibility of the data in terms of their availability or easily retrievable character, the security measures taken to restrict data appropriately and the traceability of the data to its source.

Category	DQ dimension
Intrinsic	Accuracy
	Objectivity
	Reputation
Contextual	Completeness
	Appropriate amount
	Value added
	Relevance
	Timeliness
	Actionable
Representational	Interpretable
	Easily understandable
	Consistent
	Concisely represented
	Alignment
Access	Accessibility
	Security
	Traceability

Table 1.
Data quality dimensions.

These dimensions can also be grouped into an internal and external group of dimensions. The internal group contains the dimensions that can be measured purely in terms of the data, and are generally more objective. Examples of these include the accuracy of the data, which can be examined by calculating a score on the magnitude of errors in the data or the data correctness, which can be measured through the number of errors in the data. On the other hand, the external group of dimensions evaluates how the data are related to their environment, and hence are somewhat more subjective in nature. Examples include the relevancy of data with regards to a stated objective, or their ease of understanding by the consumers of the data.

2.2 Quantitative approach

In the quantitative approach, data quality has been defined by J. M. Juran as the fitness of the data to serve a purpose in a given context, that is, in operations, decision making and/or planning as perceived by its users [1]. This concept is denoted as 'fitness for use' and is based on Juran's five principles: that is, who uses the data, how are the data used, is there a danger for human safety, what are the economic resources of the producers and users of the data and what are the characteristics taken into account by users when determining the fitness for use. This definition is widely accepted in both academic and industrial settings. However, in practice the fitness for use is a rather subjective measure as this highly depends on the users' judgement over the degree of conformity of the data to their intended use.

For example, consider the score of a student on an exam. If scores are rounded to integers, this can potentially influence the final grade that a student receives. Therefore, the rounding procedure might be accurate enough for the professors, but by rounding numbers, the students might miss out on obtaining a final grade and thus might be not accurate enough from the perspective of the student.

On the other hand, it might well be that not all uses of the data are known, neither its potential future use purposes. Therefore, DQ might be hard to evaluate using this definition.

Some definitions of data quality use the notion of zero defects, which aims to reduce defects by motivating people to prevent making mistakes by developing a constant, conscious desire to do the job right from the first time [5]. This zero-defect concept has been incorporated by P. Crosby in its Absolutes of Quality Management [6]. According to Crosby's Absolutes, data quality should conform to its requirements and prevention should be used as a manner to guarantee zero defects, which sets the performance standard. Consequently, data quality can be measured as the price of nonconformance. Although this zero-defect concept is not widely used in the data quality literature, it does emphasize again the necessity to measure data quality.

3. Measuring data quality

Based on the definitions of data quality, several DQ measurement methods have been developed, that can generally be divided into objective and subjective methods. While objective methods tend to evaluate data quality rather from the perspective of the data producer based on hard criteria, subjective methods rather take the user's perspectives and beliefs into account.

3.1 Objective DQ measurement methods

Measurements of data quality are generally intended to assess the dimensions of data quality as defined in the previous section. As a first step, a framework must be set up with the indicators that one wants to assess. Next, a proper reference for verification of the data within the data systems must be determined.

Ideally, the data are compared using real world data, which allows for validation and, if required immediate corrective actions. This method is termed ***data auditing*** and is the only way of measuring the quality level of dimensions like accuracy, completeness. Furthermore, by going through the data itself, one can discover data quality issues that were unexpected and therefore are of great value for taking corrective measures to improve data quality. However, data auditing comes at a high cost as it is very time consuming and the need of experts in the respective field is required. Furthermore, data auditing can be also very labor-intensive and requires that data controllers have access to the actual data.

For example, consider the metadata of publications that are contained in publication databases. If a data controller validates the content of the metadata fields with the metadata as indicated on the publications, inaccuracies can be detected. These can contain expected flaws like spelling errors but can also provide valuable information on unexpected errors that also might be highly relevant in the context of bibliometric analyses.

If the conditions for data auditing are not met, data controllers can use ***rule-based checking*** in order to determine data quality. This method heavily relies on business rules that are drafted based upon the domain knowledge and experience that the data controllers have with regards to the data. Consequently, these rules can only check for flaws that were anticipated by the data controllers. However, rule-based checking also offers important advantages, especially as they can be automated after conversion to validation rules, which allows for the identification of the errors (or possibly correct outliers!) via data mining techniques. Nevertheless, the presumed errors still need to be corrected, which remains labor-intensive.

3.2 Subjective DQ measurement methods

Some dimensions, however, cannot be measured objectively because of their intrinsic properties. For example, the dimension relevancy pertains to the extent to which data is applicable and helpful for the stated objective. Obviously, this dimension can only be evaluated using the ***perception of the users***. Although this results in a subjective scoring, user evaluations are the only way to measure dimensions that describe external data quality attributes. Internal data quality dimensions on the contrary are preferably measured using objective DQ measurement methods as described above.

Regardless of which methodology is chosen to measure data quality, it is always important to provide information about the measurement method and parameters in addition to the dimension under evaluation, in order that the measurement results can be interpreted correctly by everyone. Furthermore, although a lot of attention always goes to correcting errors, it is important to stress that eliminating the root cause should always be the ultimate goal [7].

4. Data quality management

4.1 Data quality frameworks

As data are extremely valuable resources in today's society, a plethora of data quality management frameworks have been published in the last decades that all strive to preserve the quality of data and to make it accessible for future use.

The most popular models are listed below, however more DQM frameworks can be found throughout the literature that show slight differences.

- DAMA DMBOK's Data governance model [8]
- EWSolutions' EIM Maturity Model [9]
- Oracle's Data Quality Management Process [10]

All frameworks are basically centered around three basic elements, that is, the metadata associated with the data, the processes involved in the registration, organization and (re)use of the data, and the organizational context in relation to the data (**Figure 1**). The quality of each individual element, as well as the interplay in between them, ultimately determines the quality and thus the true value of an organization's data heritage. Ideally, an organization uses metadata standards that are understandable throughout the organization and aligned with the organization's processes, business strategies and goals. Rather than describing all popular frameworks, we will describe critical success factors that are useful for developing effective DQ management strategies, and that can be found in all DQ frameworks.

4.2 Critical success factors

Critical success factors, also termed CSFs, have been defined by Milosevic and Patanakul as '*characteristics, conditions, or variables that can have a significant impact on the success of i.e., a company or a project when properly sustained, maintained, or managed*' [11]. In 2014, Baskarada described 11 CSFs in the field of information quality management that provide valuable means for developing effective DQ management strategies [12]. These CSFs can be clustered into four major groups, that is, training, governance, management and operational processes, that have inter-dependencies with each other.

4.2.1 Operational processes

The first group of critical success factors deals with the operational processes involved in the collection, storage, analysis and security of the data, which are all highly interdependent. As data is a valuable good, its quality should be managed throughout its entire lifecycle. In practice this comes down to taking measures that maximize, whenever possible, the **automated capture** of data in **real-time**, directly from its **original source**. This minimizes the risk of errors introduced by manual data entry, which can result in typo's, inaccuracies, missing values, erroneous data

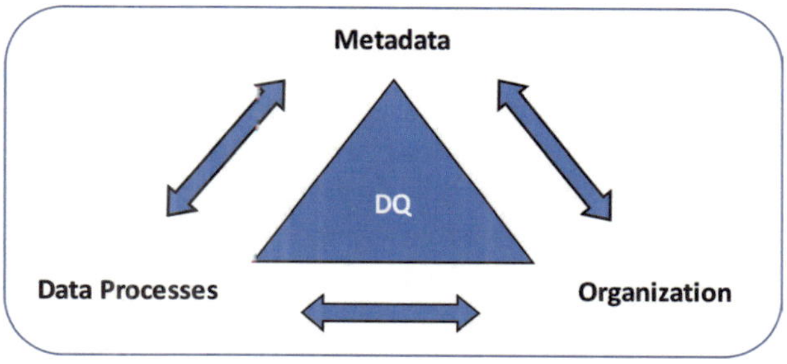

Figure 1.
The cornerstone of data quality frameworks.

due to misinterpretations, multiple copies of the same data entry. Such errors have been identified in almost all existing research and innovation databases, but have a significant impact on the resulting scientometric analyses. Suppose a highly cited paper is included in the Web of Science with typo's in the author's name. This can erroneously lead to the omission of this paper in the bibliometric analyses performed on this author, which on its turn can have a major impact on this researcher career perspectives in terms of chances of success in obtaining grants, promotion.

In addition, these errors can be due to a lack of the use of common **standards** for the concepts contained within the databases and a uniform interpretation thereof by both information providers as well consumers throughout the entire organization. Nevertheless, such standards are available, that is, the Common European Research Information Format (CERIF) is a well-known standard for exchanging research information created by the EuroCRIS organization and is widely used throughout Europe [13], the CASRAI dictionary is a standard created by the organization on Consortia Advancing Standards in Research Administration Information (CASRAI) and was created in Canada [14]. Although both communities work closely together to align the concepts and meanings described in the standards, some differences remain which might cause difficulties in exchanging information in between CRIS systems. Furthermore, the inclusion of a standard in the information model of a data system does not safeguard that all data providers use the standard similarly, nor that the data users grasp the information as intended. Next to using standards for aligning the concepts and meanings of research-related data, the formats of the data fields should be standardized as well. A well-known example here includes the various formats in which a (publication) date is recorded. By means of standardizing this format in a data system, important gains can be obtained in terms of ease of interpretation of the data, leading to more accurate analyses. However as described above, efforts should also be made to clarify what the concept of (publication) date means. For instance, it could point to the creation date, submission date, the published online date, the publication date for in print papers, the date on which the material was made available.

Furthermore, when storing research-related data, it is highly recommended to provide **traceability** to the raw data, which ensures that the data quality can always be controlled. Most bibliometric databases, including the Web of Science and Scopus, comply to this rule by providing a link to the journal article. Research data repositories mostly refer to the creator of the datasets involved. However, over time, researchers can switch positions and thus institutions and as the data are stored in institutional repositories, it would be more meaningful to refer to the research institution in question. In addition, **versioning** should be included when storing research data, as this can be very helpful to understand and potentially (re)use data. Although this is frequently observed in research data repositories, bibliometric and patent databases usually do not show version control. Finally, **back-up** and **data recovery** processes should be ensured when storing research-related data, which is mostly realized via back-up servers at various physical places.

The access to research information should be managed using an **information security management** plan in order to safeguard the intellectual property rights of the researchers that created the information, including their respective institutions. Although large data repositories on bibliometric, innovation and research data control accessibility rights, researchers themselves do not always closely follow the measures taken to control access. Particularly when it comes down to research data that may contain sensitive data [15], strict follow-up of information security measures is needed as emphasized by the EU Regulation 2016/679, also known as the General Data Protection Regulation (GDPR) that protects natural persons with regards to the processing of personal data and on the free movement of such data.

Although the GDPR regulation only applies to personal data *in se*, it nicely underpins some elements present in information security management plans.

These information security management plans indeed not only entail the accessibility rights of individuals, including user authentication and a regular update of their access rights, but also include the secure storage, archival, transmission, and if required, destruction of the information. In case of research data on natural persons, this can be achieved via pseudonymization, for example, through encryption, or via anonymization of the research information residing in data systems or on data carriers. Obviously, when transmitting research information, the proper legal agreements should be put in place, for example, non-disclosure agreements with third parties are well-known examples used to secure research information. Finally, information security management plans should also contain audit trails in order to constantly monitor and adjust the security of research-related information.

4.2.2 Management processes

A second group of CSFs encompasses the managerial processes that are imposed on these operational processes, and which are primarily aimed at the alignment of the data quality with the organization's goals with regards to the data and the resulting data analyses. Consider for example, the information requirement of a university that wants to monitor the research funds obtained via researchers. In order to answer this question, the concepts of research funds and researchers should be clear and uniform between information providers and users. Although this might seem straightforward, it could well be that the interpretation of 'researcher' is different in between stakeholders, that is, while some might include PhD students, other might omit this group. Furthermore, it could well be that the university does not have a specific label for clustering funds as belonging to the 'research' category, or that the information is only partially provided by the researchers. These examples clearly illustrate that the lack of management of operational DQ processes, has a devastating effect on the data analyses and the conclusions based thereon.

Managerial processes of data quality essentially focus on four sequential processes, that is, the determination of the information quality requirements, the assessment of the risks associated with DQ issues, the assessment or monitoring of DQ and the continuous improvement of the related DQ processes [16]. First, the **information quality requirements** should be determined of the collected data, considering all stakeholders. Next, a conceptual information model should be drafted using high-level data constructs, generally described in non-technical terms in order to be understandable by executives and managers. This model should then be translated into a logical data model that uses entities, attributes and relationships that are customized towards the organization's use of the data, in terms of the organization's terminology, semantics as well as the prevailing business rules. Finally, the logical model should be transferred to developers that can derive a physical data model in line with this logical model including validation rules, based upon the business rules, that are useful for automating data quality control. Obviously, the constructed models must consider the importance of the data within the organization. For example, certain data will be more important than others, and poor DQ of those data might have a larger negative impact in terms of loss of reputation, financial loss of the organization. The explicit **management of these DQ risks** is a must as a manner to guarantee data quality. As stated by Baskarada '*using gut feeling will result in inefficiency and an ineffective use of resources*' [16].

Next, a framework of key performance DQ indicators needs to be set up in line with the organization's goals, in order to **assess the DQ performance**. This assessment must be performed on a regular basis in order to allow for the **continuous**

improvement of data quality in terms of analyzing the root cause of the errors as well as cleansing erroneous data.

The application of such DQ managerial processes has already been implemented to some extent in CRIS systems that contain research information. For example, the Flanders Research Information Space, also termed FRIS, is a research information portal sustained by the Department of Economy, Science and Innovation in Flanders, Belgium that collects research information from a wide range of Flemish stakeholders in the research field, that is, research universities, higher education colleges, strategic research centers and research institutions (www.researchportal.be) [17]. Underlying the FRIS architecture, a conceptual metamodel was developed in order to model all concepts, attributes and relationships that are contained within FRIS. This conceptual model is based on the CERIF standard, but customized to the Flemish context. In addition, in line with the use purposes of this CRIS system, business rules were drafted to safeguard the quality of the contained information. These business rules were translated to validation rules that are used for the automated quality control of the research information received. If non-compliances to these rules are detected, the research information is rejected, and the information providers receive a notification thereby allowing for immediate data cleansing. Furthermore, the Flemish government also performs manual quality checks on a regular basis in order to validate the research information contained as validation rules in general are not well suited for detecting unpredicted errors. Such errors generally provide valuable input for root cause analyses that can identify important underlying problems which can be caused by human, process, organizational or technological factors.

4.2.3 Governance process

A third group of CSFs encompasses the governance processes associated with DQ management. These processes can be largely summarized as the **commitment of an organization's top management** to set DQ management as a priority and to stimulate a culture change throughout the entire organization in this respect. In the field of information governance, Gartner Research defined information governance as '*the specification of decision rights and an accountability framework to encourage desirable behavior in the valuation, creation, storage, use, archival and deletion of information*' [18]. In practice, information governance basically comes down to allocating budget and resources to the process of DQ management by defining roles and responsibilities, making agreements on related concepts, terms and associated DQ processes, including the monitoring, control and improvement thereof. The FRIS-system as indicated above has included data governance in order to ensure proper DQ management [17].

4.2.4 Training

Although an organization might have all operational, managerial and governance processes perfectly in place, a complete implementation of DQ management also requires the investment in training throughout the organization. A first and foremost important goal is to inform people on the importance of qualitative data to the organization. Secondly, people should receive training via training programs, course series, mentorships on the rules as set out in the operational, managerial and governance processes in order to ensure a systematic implementation of DQ throughout the entire organization. Finally, a continuous follow-up is also needed which allows for swift adjustments in case of unpredicted errors, adjustment of business rules, etc.

5. Data quality improvement

In order to safeguard the continuous monitoring of data quality and the adoption of measures to improve data quality, a DQ improvement workflow needs to be established. This workflow essentially comprises a repetitive workflow of five consecutive phases, that is, the definition, measurement, analyze, improvement and control phase as depicted in **Figure 2**. A best practice is to formalize this data quality improvement process, in terms of properly documenting all related processes and activities in each phase, as this allows for the tracking of progress throughout the entire DQ improvement workflow.

5.1 Definition of the DQ project

The DQ improvement workflow starts with defining the scope of the DQ improvement project. This includes the selection of a dataset relevant to a specific business goal, and the determination of the data attributes required. When collecting this information, it is very important to discuss the meaning of the metadata required with all stakeholders in order to be able to identify any discrepancies in interpretation of the required data attributes versus the meaning of the existing metadata, as this prevents erroneous data collection, analysis and interpretation. All obtained information should be documented using domain modeling techniques that include information on the data and the associated operations on the data [19]. Examples of such techniques include Business Process Model Notation (BPMN) diagrams [20], data flow diagrams of which the resulting information should be contained in data governance tools together with the accompanying semantics. In addition, data quality dimensions important to the specific use purposes of the data should be determined, and if possible, these are preferably defined in a measurable manner which facilitates further steps in the DQ improvement process.

For example, consider the use of bibliometric data as part of a researcher's evaluation in the context of career-wise promotions. In order to provide an adequate, qualitative data-analysis, a clear framework should be defined by an organization's management comprising what should be evaluated, that is, which publications (books, journals.), validation criteria (peer reviewed, group author.) are to be used as well as the accompanying processes. This information should be discussed with all stakeholders, that is, researchers, librarians, data analysts and IT-staff in order to harmonize the data flow, the accompanying semantics, procedures and models in accordance with the management's goals. Next, the *As Is* situation should be evaluated with regards to these intentions and according to the relevant data dimensions. In bibliometric analyses, accuracy, completeness, timeliness, relevance,

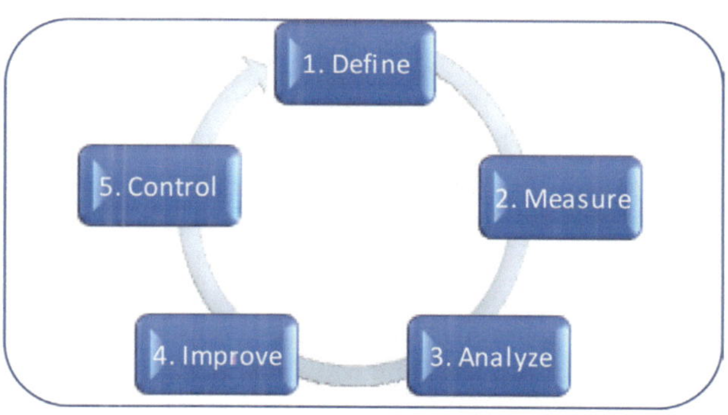

Figure 2.
Data quality improvement workflow.

accessibility, traceability of the data are all relevant dimensions, of which the accurate and complete collection and analysis of a researcher's published works are the foremost ones.

5.2 Measurement DQ

In order to determine the quality level of the current data in relation to the organization's objectives, the quality dimensions need to be expressed in a measurable manner. While the internal dimensions can be scored in a quantitative manner by means of expressing the errors in the data set in terms of magnitude, number of errors or missing records, the external dimensions are measured in a qualitative manner based on the context of the data's use purposes. Independent of the dimension under analysis, measurements must always be relevant for the purpose for which the data will be used and according to the task's requirements. Although in most cases, common sense will be used to identify task requirements, in other cases specific techniques like sensitivity analysis might be used which allows for identifying critical factors and errors in data models [21, 22]. Furthermore, data profiling is another technique frequently used in DQ assessment as a method to discover the true content, structure and quality of data by means of rule-based checking [23]. Obviously, this technique does not find all inaccurate data, as it can only identify violations to the predefined rules, and hence expected errors. For instance, data profiling can identify invalid data values (i.e., using column property analysis), invalid data combinations (i.e., through structure analysis), inaccurate data (i.e., through value rule analysis). Importantly, data profiling also provides metrics on the data inaccuracies in a dataset, that is, the number of violations, the frequency of invalid data values, etc. Such metrics can be useful as a means to communicate to stakeholders on the (in)accuracy of a data set, and the follow-up of the progression in subsequent DQ improvement programs.

In our bibliometric example, the accuracy and completeness of the bibliometric records for a given author, collected in a university's database system should be compared to a publication list provided by the author. By manually auditing the registered data found within the database system, one could indeed record the completeness of information. Furthermore, the accuracy can be tested using a manual auditing procedure. This allows for the identification of spelling errors, erroneous exchange of an author's last versus first name, etc. In addition, manual auditing also allows for identification of rather unexpected data entries, like changes in the author's first or last name over time. The latter example of a DQ inaccuracy, can however not be detected through data profiling as rule-based checking is unable to test for unexpected errors. Nevertheless, data profiling has an important role in DQ measurement as it allows for automated and thus efficient screening of DQ.

5.3 Analyzing DQ issues

Once DQ inaccuracies have been detected, these should be analyzed in order to screen for the potential existence of (groups of) common underlying root causes. For example, author names can have various problems like misspelling, last names mistaken for first names, etc. The grouping of such errors that show similar patterns, also called error cluster analysis, allows for the identification of common causes and is often more efficient in terms of time and resources as compared to handling all inaccuracies in a stand-alone way. In addition, a data event analysis can be performed which evaluates the time points when data are created and updated in order to facilitate the identification of the root causes of problems. For example, the manual entry of author names in a database system might result in misspelling, the lack of automated verification in the recording process, the lack of domain specific knowledge of the persons responsible for recording the data, ... might affect the occurrence of DQ inaccuracies.

Commonly used techniques to identify root causes include the auditing of the data, the surveying of the user perceptions and the evaluation of the data process. The identified causes can then be depicted in cause and effect diagrams, also termed Ishikawa or fishbone diagrams [24]. These diagrams cluster causes together in groups which is instrumental in identifying, classifying and prioritizing the impact of root causes to a problem. In our example root cause analysis could result in the identification of the field 'author name', as a string datatype, that is, completed according to the data provider's interpretation and accuracy. Because the datatype is set as a string, multiple inaccuracies can occur during the registration process.

5.4 DQ improvement trajectories

In the next phase, the focus resides on finding solutions to eliminate the root cause of the problem. These solutions, also termed remedies, are in fact changes to data systems or processes in order to prevent data inaccuracies from happening including the swift detection upon their occurrence. While some solutions might be oriented towards improving the data registration, others might focus on the implementation of validation rules or periodic data profiling. In addition, re-engineering of associated data processes and even training of the data provider and user community on data quality aspects, should be considered. Data cleansing might be applied as well, however this mostly is not a solution to eliminate the root cause itself.

Although solutions might be found using common sense, in most cases more efforts are needed. A frequently used method encompasses the organization of topic-oriented brainstorm sessions in the presence of all stakeholders. This approach has the benefit to tackle the problem from multiple viewpoints and at the same time enables a higher engagement of the stakeholders. Importantly, all relevant solutions to the problem should be listed and effects of the proposed solutions should be investigated carefully. In general, continuous, short-term improvements are to be preferred as these might result in quick wins which can result in additional business benefits (as DQ improvement is mostly not a goal in itself).

In our example many solutions can be found that focus on improving the correct registration of the author name. However, if an author ID would be registered and coupled to an author name, the specific focus on registering the name perfectly in a wide variety of bibliometric sources diminishes. Although this seems an easy solution at first glance, this strategy also includes the re-engineering of business processes, that is, the authentication of research publications by an author using its author ID. In order to investigate the effect of this proposed solution, one could investigate the number of publications that can be attributed to a group of authors that has registered and authenticated their research publications versus a group of authors that have no author ID (i.e., the control group) in an experimental setting. By measuring the DQ of both groups in terms of accuracy and completeness, one can see the effect of the proposed solution.

5.5 DQ control and follow-up

Based on all DQ solutions tested, the most appropriate solution(s) should be selected for implementation. It is important to note here that the success of implementation is dependent on the guidance foreseen to all stakeholders. In essence, this comes down to providing information on the solution and its effectuation on all (related) business processes to everybody involved. In addition, business rules, definitions, roles and responsibilities must be defined in consultation with all stakeholders.

Obviously, a close monitoring is needed in order to follow-up on the effectiveness of the implemented DQ solution in the real-world setting as a means to validate the (positive) impact of the proposed DQ solution. At the same time, it allows for the detection of unexpected errors that were unanticipated in the experimental test phase, and the swift adoption of corrective measure in case required. Specific monitoring tools that can be used here include control charts, also known as Shewhart charts, cause and effect diagrams, check sheets, histograms, Pareto charts, scatter diagrams, ... [25].

With regards to the author disambiguation example described, it will be required to install business processes that allow for the coupling of a unique author ID with corresponding research publications. This includes the close cooperation of the authors, research administrators, data analysts and data system/IT-staff on the definitions, business rules and responsibilities of each stakeholder. For instance, it might well be that authors are obliged to enter a unique author ID in a database system in fixed format, rather than a free text field. A business rule could be that for each author, an author ID of a given type (i.e., ORCID, Researcher ID, Scopus ID, Research Gate ID.) should be kept in a data system, which translates to a value of a given format, that is, an integer, in terms of a derived validation rule. This author ID field might be used to search large bibliometric databases such as Web of Science, Scopus, ... for publications that might be coupled to this author ID, which could be added to the bibliometric profile of a researcher. Furthermore, publications might also be retrieved using an author name search that are not yet coupled to this author ID. Therefore, an authentication step is required here in which the author has a critical responsibility to validate these publications. Research administrators and data analysts should be informed on the process of authentication in order to use the information in a correct manner. Although this might seem a perfect solution, the reality demonstrates that a continuous follow-up is required as practice demonstrates that authors sometimes use several author IDs of the same type. Therefore, a corrective action could be to adapt the business rules in order to allow for only one author ID of a give type within the data system as well as the notification to the author to take corrective measures in this respect and the follow-up thereof.

It is clear from the example described above, that data quality improvement is a process that requires continuous monitoring due to internal and external factors that might affect data quality and its related processes. Therefore, the systematic and continuous retaking of the DQ improvement workflow will be the only manner to constantly have qualitative data instrumental for high quality data analyses.

6. Conclusion

Research organizations worldwide are using data on research input and output, that is, publications, patents, research data nowadays for a wide variety of use purposes, such as evaluation, reporting and visualization of a researcher' or research organization's expertise. This places high demands on the quality of the data gathered for these purposes, which have—in most cases—largely outgrown the initial intentions when the data systems were constructed. Moreover, the research world has evolved in a global, dynamic manner in which research data are increasingly being used in order to monitor the efficiency of research processes, the research productivity and even strategic decision making. In order to safeguard correct data analysis, research-related data must be assessed on all relevant quality dimensions, and inaccuracies must be addressed using data quality improvement trajectories as discussed in this chapter. The integration of a data quality management policy, is the only way to ensure the fitness for use of research-related data for various applications and business processes across the research world as the impact of inaccurate date can have tremendous effects on a researcher's or research organization's future prospects.

Acknowledgements

This work is carried out by the Expertise Centre for Research and Development Monitoring (ECOOM) in Flanders, which is supported by the Department of Economy, Science and Innovation, Flanders.

A. Abbreviations

BPMN	Business Process Model Notation
CASRAI	Consortia Advancing Standards in Research Administration Information
CERIF	Common European Research Information Format
CRIS	current research information systems
FRIS	Flanders Research Information Space
DQ	data quality
DQM	data quality management

Author details

Sadia Vancauwenbergh
ECOOM-Hasselt and Hasselt University, Hasselt, Belgium

*Address all correspondence to: sadia.vancauwenbergh@uhasselt.be

References

[1] Juran JM, Blanton Godfrey A. Juran's Quality Handbook. 7th ed. Europe: McGraw-Hill Education; 2016. p. 992. ISBN-10: 9781259643613

[2] Wang RY, Strong DM. Beyond accuracy: What data quality means to data consumers. Journal of Management Information Systems. 1996;**12**(4):5-33. DOI: 10.1080/07421222.1996.11518099

[3] Moges H-T, Dejaeger K, Lemahieu W, Baesens B. A total data quality management for credit risk: New insights and challenges. International Journal of Information Quality. 2012;**3**(1):1-27. DOI: 10.1504/IJIQ.2012.050036

[4] Culnan M. The dimensions of accessibility to online information: Implications for implementing office information systems. ACM Transactions on Office Information Systems. 1984;**2**(2):141-150. DOI: 10.1145/521.523

[5] Halpin JF. Zero Defects: A New Dimension in Quality Assurance. New York City: McGraw-Hill; 1966. p. 228. OCLC 567983091

[6] Crosby PB. 8: Quality Improvement Program. Quality Is Free: The Art of Making Quality Certain. New York City: McGraw-Hill; 1979. pp. 127-139. ISBN 9780070145122. OCLC 3843884

[7] Redman TC. Data Quality: The Field Guide. 1st ed. Boston: Digital Press; 2001. 256 p. ISBN-10 1555582516

[8] DAMA International. The DAMA Guide to the Data Management Body of Knowledge (DAMA-DMBOK). 2nd ed. Bradley Beach: Technics Publications, LLC; 2009. 430 p. ISBN-10: 0977140083

[9] EWSolutions, Foundations of Enterprise Data Management [Internet]. 2013. Available from: https://www.ewsolutions.com/foundations-enterprise-data-management/ [Accessed: 18 April 2019]

[10] Oracle, Oracle Warehouse Builder Users Guide 10g Release 2(10.2.0.2) [Internet]. 2009. Available from: https://docs.oracle.com/cd/B31080_01/doc/owb.102/b28223/concept_data_quality.htm [Accessed: 18 April 2019]

[11] Milosevic D, Patanakul P. Standardized project management may increase development projects success. International Journal of Project Management. 2005;**23**:181-192. DOI: 10.1016/j.ijproman.2004.11.002

[12] Baskarada S, Koronios A. A critical success factor framework for information quality management. Information Systems Management. 2014;**31**(4):276-295. DOI: 10.1080/10580530.2014.958023

[13] EuroCRIS, CERIF: Main features of CERIF. Available from: https://www.eurocris.org/cerif/main-features-cerif [Accessed: 18 April 2019]

[14] CASRAI: CASRAI dictionary. Available from: https://dictionary.casrai.org/Main_Page [Accessed: 19 April 2019]

[15] European Commission: Sensitive data. Available from: https://ec.europa.eu/info/law/law-topic/data-protection/reform/rules-business-and-organisations/legal-grounds-processing-data/sensitive-data_en [Accessed: 19 April 2019]

[16] European Commission: Data protection in the EU. Available from: https://ec.europa.eu/info/law/law-topic/data-protection/data-protection-eu_en [Accessed: 19 April 2019]

[17] Vancauwenbergh S, De Leenheer P, Van Grootel G. On research information and classification governance in an

inter-organizational context: The Flanders Research Information Space. Scientometrics. 2016;**108**(1):425-439. DOI: 10.1007/s11192-016-1912-7

[18] Bell T, Logan D, Friedman T. Key issues for establishin information governance policies, processes and organization. Gartner Research; 2008

[19] Fowler M. Patterns of Enterprise Application Architecture. 1st ed. Crawfordsville: Addison Wesley; 2003. 116 p. ISBN-10: 0321127420

[20] White SA. Process Modeling Notations and Workflow Patterns. Newton: Business Process Trends; 2004:1-24. Available from: http://www.bptrends.com/publicationfiles/03-04%20WP%20Notations%20and%20Workflow%20Patterns%20-%20White.pdf

[21] Saltelli A. Sensitivity analysis for importance assessment. Risk Analysis. 2002;**22**(3):1-12. DOI: 10.1111/0272-4332.00040

[22] Saltelli A, Ratto M, Andres T, Campolongo F, Cariboni J, Gatelli D, et al. Global Sensitivity Analysis: The Primer. Chichester: John Wiley & Sons; 2008. 305 p. ISBN-10: 0470059974

[23] Woodall P, Oberhofer M, Borek A. A classification of data quality assessment and improvement methods. International Journal of Information Quality. 2014;**3**(4):298-321. DOI: 10.1504/ijiq.2014.068656

[24] Ishikawa K. Guide to quality control. 1st ed. Tokyo: Asian Productivity Organization; 1976. 226 p. ISBN: 92-833-1036-5

[25] Tague NR. The Quality Toolbox. Milwaukee, Wisconsin: American Society for Quality; 2005. p. 15. ISBN-10: 0873896394

Chapter 2

Advantages and Disadvantages of the Webometrics Ranking System

Suad Kunosić, Denis Čeke and Enver Zerem

Abstract

Today, there are several well-known global ranking lists for ranking universities in the world. While some of them ranked only a few hundreds of best and most influential universities, there are those that include a much larger number of ranking scientific institutions. One such global list which ranks the largest number of scientific institutions and scientists in the world is called Webometrics list. This list is very important for less developed economies and developing countries which have not established a sufficient quality control system of higher education quality, so this list serves as a corrective to the international evaluation of a wide range of universities in the world. In such a complex IT system of ranking an extremely large number of institutions and scientists, this system shows some disadvantages when ranking, which of course can be overcome by introducing certain improvements within the system of ranking. Systems that perform the collection, analysis, and indexing data have their advantages and disadvantages, which can sometimes lead to a misinterpretation of the data collected. Among other things, we will consider the possible solutions which would improve the rating system and prevent possible manipulation and uncertainty in the presentation of current and final results ranking.

Keywords: webometrics, university ranking systems, ranking scientists, university science transparency, web crawler, web scraping, Internet bot

1. Introduction

According to the definition by Björneborn and Ingwersen [1, 2], webometrics represents a joint (synergy) activity, i.e., application of other two approaches in one element known as bibliometrics and informetrics, for researching of the web, its information resources, structure, and technologies.

The name "webometrics" was defined in 1997, and it was created and established by Tomas Almind and Peter Ingwersen with an intention to show that informetric analysis can be applied to the web as an important source for measuring values (weight/sense) of documents and information [3]. They suggested several specific informetric parameters such as hyperlinks per website and sensitivity of links on websites distributed via types of documents and names of domains. Björneborn and Ingwersen [1] defined webometrics as "The study of the quantitative aspects of the construction and use of information resources, structures and technologies on the Web, drawing on bibliometrics and informetrics approach." One developed a detailed topology of links, a diagram of nodes on the web, and additional terminology [4]. The area of activity and what webometrics includes may, in a wider sense, be characterized as (a) website content analysis, (b) web technology analysis, (c) web usage analysis, and web link structure analysis. Researches in this field imply creation of new discoveries based on analyses of numbers and types of hyperlinks, structure of the World Wide Web, and patterns of usage of the web as a mass communication medium and exchange of information.

Another definition of webometrics was given by *Mike Thelwall* in 2004, "... the study of web-based content with primarily quantitative methods for social science research goals using techniques that are not specific to one field of study," which underlines development of applied methods for usage in a wider scope of social sciences. The purpose of this alternative definition was not to replace the primary definition within Information Science [5] but to support publishing of appropriate methods out of the scope of the Information Science.

After these events, Ingwersen represented Web Impact Factor (WIF) [6] in 1998, which represented a key metrics to measure and analyze hyperlinks of websites.

Basically, WIF measure may be defined as a number of sites of a certain web host (website) or portals referred to by links from other websites or web hosts, divided with the number of shared/published websites on that web host which are available to the web/web robots.

Namely, it was logical to assume that areas of great interest would attract more sequential links than average. The greatest advantage of WIF, in which logic was inherited from significance of quoting within an impact factor of a journal, was that it was easy to calculate with the application of advanced inquiries of a browser represented by AltaVista, a leading commercial search engine of that time.

However, usage of WIF measure was neglected after comprehensive analyses and obtained results, due to mathematical artifacts obtained from mathematical law, i.e., due to *power law distributions* of these variables. Other similar indicators which applied a size of an institution instead of a number of websites showed as much more useful for the purpose of analyses.

Subsequently, analyses of links were more directed toward analyses of influence of links and analyses of net connectedness of links, taking into consideration quantity of links as a reflection of productivity of researching within academic and scientific space.

Webometrics gradually evolved and became a great coherent field within the Information Science, at least from bibliometric perspective [7, 8], including analyses of links, web quotations, and a range of other web-based quantitative techniques.

Hyperlinks on websites are structured similarly like quotations in academic (scientific) journals since they guide from a source document to the final document. Similarity of links and quotations, together with the fact that universities were among the first ones which massively started applying advantages of the web, resulted in the appearance of numerous important naturally imposed research objectives. Such sequence of events imposed the question whether it was possible to use hyperlinks in a similar way as academic quotations or quotes in journals and articles, the question of validity of usage of a number of links and data obtained by AltaVista browser in the research and the best way to count links [9]. Simultaneously with these analyses of links, other researchers from the field of Information Science researched reliability and coverage of an area of browsing by browsers and change in contents of the web itself or individual collections of websites [10]. These three types of researches related to measuring the web are all together called webometrics.

Among other things, webometrics has become a useful methodology in many other fields, such as creation of ranking of universities in the world based on webometrics [11, 12], for scientometric evaluations or researches in some scientific fields [13].

2. Webometrics methodology

Webometrics methodology includes analyses of links, analyses of web quotations, evaluations of results of browsing via web browsers, as well as some basic descriptive studies and analyses of the web [15].

The web is of great importance as a communication medium, i.e., a platform for placing and archiving a wide spectrum of documents. A significant number of repositories of various kinds of documents are related to the academic society, and therefore application of this methodology in general ranking of a current situation in the academic field is more significant. Because of this huge and easily accessible source of information, unlimited possibilities for measuring or counting contents of the web turned up in a wide range (e.g., a number of web hosts or a number of websites) or in a narrower range (e.g., a number of web locations in a state, a number of web pages on a website of a university).

Although the terms “Internet” and “web” are usually treated as synonyms, they are not the same. Namely, the “Internet” represents a global network of computers which can share information, while the term “web” specifically refers to a group of interrelated documents available for review and downloading using HTTP [14].

For an analysis of the system of ranking of universities, Webometrics Ranking, the most important parts of webometrics methodology would be link analysis and web browser analysis, i.e., a survey of ways in which relevant information that are used in the ranking process of universities according to the Webometrics ranking methodology may be obtained.

2.1 Link analysis

Link analysis is a quantitative study of hyperlinks among websites [15]. Similar to a mechanism of counting of quoted works in journals and articles, the importance of websites can be evaluated with links and their analysis. As previously mentioned, the importance or influence of a website on the Internet is defined as Web Impact Factor [5], which, obviously, is similar to the concept of an impact factor of a journal (*Journal Impact Factor, JIF*).

The idea behind the link analysis is that one can practically assume that a number of links pointing to (guiding toward another location) the academic space of a web content can be proportional to productivity of a research of an organization at the level of a university [9], departments [16], research groups [17], or individual researches [18].

Calculation of WIF [19] can be obtained as a logic amount of a number of links, i.e., external or incoming links (*inlinks*) toward a website divided by a number of sites of a certain web host in a certain moment of time. Further information regarding the calculation of WIF is to be looked for in the work [6, 19].

2.2 Webometrics tools for collection of data from the Internet

Web tools such as search engines, web crawlers, and webometrics software which are used for collecting data from the web are called *Webometrics tools* [5].

The area of research in the field of webometrics can, in a wider sense, be divided into the following segments:

- Analysis of contents of websites
- Analysis of web technologies
- Analysis of application of web contents
- Analysis of structure of web links

To analyze data for the needs of webometrics, it is very important to know the source of information for each of the mentioned categories of webometrics. The main role of web browsers is to grasp relevant information on the basis of specific inquiries from various (heterogenous) sources of information.

Basically, there are two categories of sources of information which can be used in the research of webometrics:

- Commercial web search engines
- Personal web crawlers

Web search engines are computer programs which, on the basis of special algorithms, find appropriate information on the web, index them, and place them into databases appropriated for those purposes.

From the point of view of the webometrics research, web search engines can fundamentally be divided into two categories:

- Web search engines which support searches related to the field of webometrics
- Web search engines of a general type which do not have any additional capacity to direct searches toward terms related to the field of webometrics

Web search engines, such as Google, Yahoo, and Bing, enable users to access a vast quantity of information related to contents and structure of links on the web free of charge. Web browsers collect information in a similar manner as web crawlers which are used by users to collect linked data. Basically, web browsers contain three different parts, crawler, indexer, and interface, in which one enters inquiries with terms to be browsed [10]. Led by this fact, authors Aquillo et al. [11] applied advanced options of web browsers to collect data from the web for the needs of ranking of universities.

Web crawlers are programs with the main objective to collect data from precisely defined web locations. They function in the following way: they start collecting data from a certain web location, and then they apply links contained by that web location so that a web crawler could move automatically and independently to a next processed web location, from one site to another until there are several links to be monitored and analyzed.

Regardless of the existence of some additional tools for analysis of links such as *LinkDiscoverer* [20], *SocSciBot* [21], and *Webometric Analyst/LexiURL Searcher* [22], Thelwall and Sud [23] underlined that researchers still depended on *application programming interface* (API) of commercial browsers for collection of raw data for their webometric studies. These API functions enable automatic data collection and enable programmers to encrypt programs with which one can access results of browsing. Yahoo canceled its *free-of-charge* support for usage of API functions for the purpose of browsing, Google has limited access to its API from 2011, and Bing also has limited a *free-of-charge* access to API 2.0 from 2012. This essentially canceled or significantly limited possibilities to collect important information for extensive researches within the field of webometrics. Although web browsers have a very important role in data collection, none of them is able to collect data from the whole web. The web is a dynamic environment, and there are fluctuations in the results obtained by browsing.

Generally speaking, one can say that web crawlers are an essentially better tool than web browsers if one talks about researches about the webometrics.

2.2.1 Data collection with commercial search engines

The most popular web search engines, which are very popular besides their application in the webometrics, are Google, Yahoo, and Bing. Each of the web search engines uses its own algorithms for browsing and different techniques for indexing and browsing of the web. Actually, it means that if a user wants to enter an inquiry into a search engine in a form of, for example, "webometrics methodology," there is a huge probability that he/she would obtain different results from different search engines for the same browsed term. These algorithms applied by the web search engines are business secrets of corporations standing behind their implementation. Besides the abovementioned search engines, there are other search engines, but these three are the most popular due to the quality of obtained results and speed of browsing. In application of some of web engines, there are some keywords for browsing that may be entered so that obtained results could be filtered and oriented toward a searched term. For example, if one enters the term "site:untz.ba" in Google search engine, the inquiry will provide us all data related to that domain, its auxiliary subdomains, and all sites indexed by the browser.

Furthermore, if one enters a string in the form of "site:untz.ba <space> filetype:pdf," the browser would provide us all sites and subdomains containing documents of *Adobe Portable Document Format* (Adobe PDF) type and a direct link to the same. These examples are specifically applicable to Google search engine.

Web search engines of the Internet are very important in researching of the field of webometrics because their databases are a source of information that cover a great part of data of the web. Although commercial search engines are very important for surfing the Internet and data collection, they have some significant limitations, among which the following stand out:

- Web search engines do not index the whole web space [24, 10, 19].
- Systems for ranking of results of browsing eliminate similar or identical sites in results of browsing with an objective to eliminate useless information [25, 26].
- Algorithms that search engines use for surfing the web and generation of reports are corporative business secrets, and, therefore, an exact criterium for collection, sorting, and ranking information by importance is not known [19].
- A total result obtained in a search by a web search engine is assessed by time necessary for a search rather than by thoroughness and going into details into accurateness of data since they apply an algorithm which performs prioritization [4].
- Results may be conditioned by a national or a language area [27].
- Results may fluctuate and change from time to time.

Regardless of their limitations, commercial web search engines are one of the unique and best sources of information which are currently available but only for certain types of webometrics researches. At the same time, they are not properly designed for the purpose necessary for the academic community, and results usually are not thorough enough, which would be a great need of this field [28].

If an interface of a web browser is directly used for browsing, data collection may be a very demanding process in regard to time. This problem may be overcome with an application of a special software based on application program interface developed by companies which create web search engines and other services on the web.

2.2.2 Web crawlers as a source of data

Another important source of data is personal *web crawlers*. Among the most popular free-of-charge tools of this type, which are used to analyze links, are *SocSciBot* [21] and *LexiURL* [29]. Both of these *crawlers* are developed by Professor Mike Thelwall from the University of Wolverhampton, UK, in order to find alternative strategies and methods to analyze links. The essence of functioning of these tools is that they search for and download certain websites from the web and analyze them with an integrated analytical software, such as *Pajek* [30], *Ucinet* [31], *NetDraw* [32], etc., for the purpose of data analysis and creation of a graph of a network representing a scheme of data linking.

2.2.3 Challenges within the webometrics research field

Webometrics functions on a principle of an analysis of academic and non-academic articles. Academic documents include publications such as e-journals, e-books, patents, technical reports, etc. Nonacademic documents include websites—commercial ones, sites of social networks, etc.—published by individuals, blogs, and portals where there is not any (i.e., which process of publishing of contents does not comply with) *peer-reviewed* system. The greatest challenges within the webometrics research field are in finding relevant sources of data and in the development and implementation of techniques for their efficient collection. Among the four research fields within webometrics, link analysis has been in the focus more and more since most of the commercial web search engines canceled their support related to browsing the web contents which include link analysis. For these reasons, there is still a great need for alternative sources of data.

2.3 Alternative sources of data

In the first decade of the twenty-first century, most of the web search engines supported the webometrics research filed with application of special keywords for search engines such as "site:domain," "linkdomain," "linkfromdomain," etc. Starting from 2012 there has been a great change which has reflected the field of usage of sources of data for webometrics researches as a *matter of policy* which was started by owners of the web search engines. As a result of the mentioned, most of the web search engines canceled their support to the webometrics. Researchers from the field of webometrics tended to find alternative sources of data to go on with their researches. A survey of some of the existing systems by which data may be collected for the needs of webometrics analysis is given hereafter.

Alexa Internet [33] was established in 1996. As a *search engine optimization* (SEO) tool, Alexa collects data on the basis of behavior of users on the web, while they visit some sites using their analytic tool. The data are analyzed in a manner to give information for a global ranking or ranking within a country. One also analyzes data related to web communication and a total number of sites which refer to a certain web domain, etc.

Alexa Toolbar Service [34] is a smaller software application which collects and stores information about websites, web domains, and other sites which this tool uses to collect data regarding analyses of users.

In 2005 *Who.is* [35] become a web portal for searching for and collection of data about web domains of any organization or institution. Who.is offered a unique tool to obtain information about IP addresses, locations of domains, DNS names of servers, information related to availability of domains, and information related to various organizations or universities which belonged or belong to those institutions.

Webconfs.com [36] represents one of the additional tools which may be used as a source of data for webometrics researches.

Majestic SEO tool [37] represents one of the best tools related to analyses of *back-link*, *incoming link*, *inbound link*, *inlink*, and *inward link*. Backlink for an assessed web resource is a link which shows a hyperlink from some other web location to the observed web location. A web resource may be a web host, a website, or a web directory. Backlinks are one of the indicators of popularity of a website, and they represent a very significant source of information. A rank or value of a site within a web domain increases depending on the quality of *backlinks*.

Searchmetrics [38] is a professional SEO tool which enables a survey of all data related to visibility and social visibility of websites. Visibility of a site is analyzed through *PageRank* [39], which is a tool for analysis of *metatags*. Afterward one analyzes a server and a domain where a certain content is located (domain's age, domain's popularity, reverse IP addresses), if there are tools for analyses of links (popularity of a link, counter of backlinks, value of links, exit links). Visibility of social data is related to links related to social networks such as *Facebook*, *Twitter*, *LinkedIn*, and *Google+*.

Ahrefs.com [40] is a famous set of tools (Site Explorer [41], Content Explorer [42], Keywords Explorer [43], Rank Tracker [44], Site Audit [45]) for analyzing backlinks to the websites, and it is a very important tool for SEO analyses.

3. University ranking systems

These days, the Internet has become the main source of scientific information, both for the academic community and for the society. The whole society has been turning to the Internet as a primary medium for presentation of information to the public. On that ground, the fact that web publications are a primary tool for communication within the educational system and that they reflect the complete picture of quality and performances of universities has become very important [51]. Bearing in mind the development of digital world, the influence of electronic publications is significantly greater than the influence of written media or printed versions of journals and books today. Websites are the cheapest and the most efficient way to stimulate all of the three academic missions: to educate, to research, and to transfer knowledge [51]. This fact is one of the main reasons why web data have been extensively used for evaluation, inter alia, of universities and research institutions in the last couple of years.

Ranking is a process in which one defines positions of elements in a group in regard to a total system so that for any two elements in a sequence, the first one is ranked "as higher than," "as lower than," or "as equal to" the second item of a sequence [46].

Ranking process appears in many fields whether they are academic or of other type. In a case of academic space, ranking may be applied in different parts of academic space, starting from ranking of professors and ranking of researchers and research centers to ranking of universities. Ranking of universities is an especially interesting field of application of ranking.

Currently, one implements a process of comparing and evaluating universities in the domain of academic and research performances with the existing system of ranking of universities. Most of the academic institutions rely on data obtained from the ranking system of universities which serve them as indicators of a progress of an institution over time in regard to other academic institutions [47]. Besides this, information from these ranking lists often serve as a basis for applying for and obtaining financial assets from founders or other institutions on the basis of a position on these lists [48]. On the other hand, potential beneficiaries of services of a university use these lists to evaluate academic institutions to decide which one to attend and to evaluate which one provides better options for education and further employment.

The study [47] identified 24 ranking systems. Thirteen ranking systems were analyzed into details since their lists were active during the last couple of years, i.e., from 2015 to 2016. Other ranking systems were excluded from further analysis because they did not publish information and did not include indicators of their performances or published their ranking methodologies. The study evaluated between 500 and 5000 institutions. The oldest ranking system, *Carnegie Classification*, was established in 1973. All other ranking systems were first published between 2003 and 2015. The study mentioned that three ranking systems were led by universities, two were led by agencies, five by consultancy or independent groups, and one was led by an institution established by a government.

In the analysis from the study [47], 4 systems for ranking out of 13 for evaluation claimed that they used their results to evaluate quality or performances of researches. Nine of thirteen systems use a total number of publications as an indicator for evaluation of quality or performances of researches—this is usually defined as a number of *peer-reviewed* articles from bases of Thomson Reuters' Web of Science Core Collections or SCOPUS which is maintained by Elsevier. On average, 33.8% ranking results are ascribed to publications and quotations or to various versions of these metrics [47].

Ranking systems that strongly rely on metrics related to publications and quotations are *Leiden Ranking*, *Shanghai*, *SCImago*, *URAP*, *US News and World Report*, and *EU U-Multirank* systems. The fact that SCImago ranking system takes the presence on the web into consideration by Google metrics [49], which is 20% of the total result of ranking, is very interesting. Similarly, Webometrics ranking list includes all universities of the world which are present on the web in the ranking system. The objective of this list is to encourage universities and their personnel to increase visibility of universities through creating more websites of university organizations and institutions. A survey of percentual participation and application of individual indicators applied by various systems is given in the work into details [47]. According to [47] current indicators are not adequate for an accurate assessment of results of researches, and they need to be amended and expanded to satisfy a standardized criterium.

3.1 Webometrics Ranking of World Universities

Several research teams have been working on the development of web indicators since the mid-1990s. Realizing possibilities of this kind of ranking, the European Commission started several projects for this purpose: EICSTES (www.eicstes.org—currently inactive), WISER (www.wiserweb.org—currently inactive), and www.webindicators.org (currently inactive).

After noting capabilities and importance of web search engines as the main agent to access information being processed and being processed by the web [53], one created new indicators [54, 11] which should have been milestones to solve problems arising from instability of results of browsing via web search engines [55] and artifacts arising from calculation of Web Impact Factors [6] [51].

The first catalogs of universities were created with projects EICSTES and WEISER, and the first preliminary list of these universities based on web indicators was published in 2004. This application of cybermetrics or webometrics techniques did not significantly differ from similar scientometric proposals where bibliometric data were the basis of information used in analyses [56, 51].

Most of the bibliometric indicators, such as a number of publications or quotations, are easily available. However, the problem with such access is that in this way only a limited number of information about activities, researchers, and observed institutions are available since only formal publications are taken into consideration. Actually, scientometric tasks should contain more elements, and more variables should be added [51].

However, including additional elements in an analysis, particularly when they are not easily available, may complicate the analysis and sometimes may be inapplicable when it comes to a global work plan. Among other things, there is an attitude that publications are not the only indicator of evaluation of professors. There are, inter alia, materials for lectures, raw data, slides from lectures, software, and bibliographic or linked lists (bookmarks), which are also deemed as relevant information about a professor's dedication to students [51].

Besides these data, a structure and a content of all kinds of administrative information provided by an institution also have their value. All these elements speak for themselves when published publicly in the virtual world, the web world, and are very good indicators of an academic level of an educational institution. The fact that if someone is not on the web she/he does not exist supports the previous statement. Web space provides a comprehensive way to describe a wide range of activities of an institution where scientific publications represent only one of components which may be found on websites.

Today, highly ranked researchers, institutions, and universities publish millions of pages with various materials composed of hundreds of departments and services, hundreds of research teams, and thousands of students on their websites.

Until now one has talked about webometrics methodology and systems for ranking of universities generally. However, the topic of this chapter is oriented toward a specific system of ranking of universities which applies webometrics methodology for the world's ranking of universities. This chapter will elaborate on Webometrics Ranking of World Universities, which was developed by and is under the competence of Cybermetrics Lab (Spanish National Research Council, CSIC) [50], who developed indicators called web ranking (WR) for the ranking process and who initially considered the following elements in the ranking process [51]: a number of published websites (S); a number of files contained, including PDF, ps, doc, and PPT form of documents (R); a number of articles collected via Google Scholar (GS) database system (Sc); and a total number of external links (V).

Webometrics Ranking of World Universities is the largest list for academic ranking of higher education institutions. From 2004, Cybermetrics Lab has implemented an independent, objective, free, open scientific exercise for provision of reliable, multidimensional, updated, and useful information about performances of universities from all over the world on the basis of their presence and impact on the web every 6 months.

Cybermetrics Lab has been developing quantitative studies on the Academic Web Network since the mid-1990s. The first indicator was introduced during the EASST/4S conference in Bielefeld (1996), and collection of web data from European universities started in 1999 with a support of EICSTES project financed by the European Union.

These efforts are a continuation of scientometric research Cybermetrics Lab which started in 1994 and which was presented on a conference of the International Society for Scientometrics and Informetrics (ISSI, 1995–2011) and International Conferences on Scientific and Technology Indicators (STI-ENID, 1996–2012) and published in journals with a great impact effect (*Journal of Informetrics*, *Journal of American Society for Information Science and Technology*, *Scientometrics*, *Journal of Information Science*, *Processing Information and Management*, *Research Assessment*, and others). In 1997 one started issuing journal *Cybermetrics* dedicated to published works about webometrics.

After publishing of ranking of the University of Jiao Tong in Shanghai, Academic Ranking of World Universities (ARWU) [52] in 2003, team Cybermetrics Lab decided to approve the main innovations proposed by Liu and his team. It was suggested that ranking should be done on a basis of publicly available web data, combining variables in a composite directory and with a real global coverage. The first edition was published in 2004, and it has been issued two times a year since 2006. After 2008 the portal has included webometrics ranking for research centers, hospitals, repositories, and business schools.

3.1.1 Composite indicator

Probably one of the most important contributions of *Shanghai* ranking was introduction of the **composite indicator**, which combines a system of weighing factors with a set of indicators. Traditional bibliometric indexes are made on ratios such as Garfield's journal impact factor which is based on variables which follow the power law and are useless for description of huge and complicated scenarios.

Ingwersen's proposal from 1998 [6] for a similarly designed *Web Impact Factor* which uses ratio *links/websites* (L/W) was equally useless due to mathematical artifacts which it generates.

Following the *Shanghai* model up, Cybermetrics Lab developed an indicator which transforms relation L/W into the following formula $aL + bW$, where L and W should be normalized in advance and a and b are weights which add 100%. Cybermetrics Lab strongly discouraged the usage of WIF due to its serious disadvantages. The composite indicator may be designed with different groups of variables and weights according to the needs of programmers and models. Webometrics applies "a priori" scientific model for the creation of a composite indicator. Other ranking lists chose arbitrary weights for very dependable variables and even combine raw values *with ratios.* None of them follows up a logic relation among variables related to activities and influential variables, i.e., each group represents 50% out of the total measure of weight.

Values should be normalized before any combination of variables, but the practice of application of percentage is mainly inaccurate due to *power law* distribution of data.

Webometrics *log* normalizes variables before combining in the ratio of 1:1 between activity/presence and visibility/influence of a group of indicators.

3.1.2 Collection of data for webometrics ranking

Collection of a great quantity of data from the Internet, where one has to go through thousands of sites, may be done only automatically. One of the possibilities is to use commercial or free-of-charge crawlers, but adjustment of such systems for adjusted needs may be a complicated and difficult task, and it requires a significant participation of human and computer resources [57]. On the other hand, web search engines already have well-designed and tested systems for this need, and they do regular updates of their databases and have many tools which enable automatization of work so that machines may be easily adjusted to extract required data. Furthermore, web search engines are the main agents in navigation process on the web, and therefore the presence of a web domain in their databases represents an indicator of visibility on the Internet. Commercial web search engines also have limitations, which often include inconsistent and rounded-off results of browsing, favoritism in geographic and language coverage of results of browsing, or frequent and nontransparent changes in their work procedures. Due to the mentioned problems, one uses several web search engines together in practice, when collecting data. The most popular search engines such as Google (and Google Scholar), Yahoo Search, Bing, Exalead, and Alexa [11] are used for these purposes.

3.1.3 The webometrics ranking weighing model

Webometrics ranking system [58] performs an evaluation and ranking of universities of the world two times a year (January/February and June/July) by its own developed methodology. Webometrics ranking methodology includes several phases and applies several systems so that data necessary for ranking and analyses may be updated and collected in time.

According to [51], there are three key aspects that need to be measured in the academic web space:

- Size, i.e., quantity of published information
- Visibility, number of certain cases of appearance on other web hosts which refer to the analyzed web host (quotations of websites-hosts = number of external incoming links) obtained by a domain
- Popularity, which represents a number of visits to a website

Bibliometrics has traditionally ignored frequency of appearance of a journal on various locations or sources of data and has focused on an impact of a journal, i.e., relation between a number of quotations and a number of published articles in the journal. A similar approach was proposed in the case of Webometrics ranking.

Webometrics ranking performs monitoring of a certain group of parameters (criteria) (**Table 1**), but only size and visibility of a web host are included in the

Criteria	Indicator	Sources	Weight
Size	Number of pages (*S*)	Google, Yahoo, Live, Exalead	25%
	Number of rich files (PDF, PPT, DOC, and PS) (*R*)	Google	12.5%
	Number of papers (*Sc*)	Google Scholar	12.5%
Visibility	Number of external links (*V*)	Yahoo, Exalead, Live	50%
Luminosity	Number of external outlinks		
Subdomains	Number of subdomains		
Popularity	Number of visits		

Table 1.
Criteria and weights used in the calculation of the WR indicator [51].

final data which are used for ranking. A model for ranking defines that a relation between these two parameters (size and visibility) is taken in the ratio 1:1. In order to take diversity of academic activities and services into consideration, component "size" is divided into three parts so that one could measure raw data about a quantity of websites, a number of rich files, and a number of articles and publications collected by Google Scholar system.

According to the work [51], criteria and weights used for calculation of WR indicators in those times were obtained from several sources only, which mainly were web search engines. Some of those search engines are not used to obtain data any more, but there are some new search engines together with some of the old ones which improved their algorithms for indexing and browsing of results from the web.

Pursuant to the proposed model, ranking (web ranking) is calculated with the following equation (Eq. (1)):

$$WR = 2 \times Rank(S) + 1 \times Rank(R) + 1 \times Rank(Sc) + 4 \times Rank(V) \quad (1)$$

The ratio which combines weights ascribed to each of the elements is (2 + 1 + 1):4 or 1:1, which was the initial intention. In order to avoid problems related to size, search engine bias, and other factors, results collected in this way, which initially were expressed as absolute values of numbers, are log-normalized and transformed into ordinal numbers and then combined with the previously mentioned equation for WR [59].

Over the years of application of the system, Cybermetrics Lab has made adjustments of indicators of calculation according to the analyses of data available during the years preceding the analyses. The data shown in tables on www.webometrics.info are basically ranks (smaller number, better ranking) which purpose is to show individual performances, but one has to bear in mind that those values are not applied in ranking calculations [60].

Due to technical problems in the previous versions of the ranking system, Cybermetrics Lab changed some of the ranking weights (presence and excellence from **Table 2**) in the last version of the ranking system so that the current methodology is shown in **Table 2** (January edition, 2019.1.0.).

Indicators	Description	Source	Weight
Presence	Size (number of web pages) of the main web domain of the institution. It includes all the subdomains sharing the same (central or main) web domain and all the file types including rich files like PDF documents	*Google*	5%
Visibility (or impact)	Number of external networks (subnets) originating backlinks to the institution's webpages After normalization, the average value between the two sources is selected	*Ahrefs, Majestic*	50%
Transparency (or openness)	Number of citations from top authors according to the source	*Google Scholar Citations*	10%
Excellence (or scholar)	Number of papers among the top 10% most cited in 26 disciplines Data for the 5-year period (2012–2016)	*SCImago*	35%

Table 2.
Webometrics university ranking methodology (January edition, 2019.1.0.) [60].

3.1.4 Several relevant facts about webometrics ranking of universities

Results of ranking of universities [58] have been published two times a year since 2004 (data are collected during the first week of January and July to be prepared and published in the end of both of the months) covering more than 28,000 institutions of higher education all over the world with their analyses.

The data are collected between January 1 and January 20, depending on a current edition of a ranking publication. Data are taken (sampled) for each of the variables at least two times during the certain period, and the greatest value is taken as the final value to be analyzed in order to avoid possible errors in data collection. Inconsistency of web search engines is very huge so that the obtained results may be diversified, and there is a small possibility for their replication if browsing is done several days later. Google is very geographically biased; that is why data are collected with *google.com* mirror related to the domain, and English is used for the interface and Madrid (Spain) as the location.

A final publishing of ranking data is performed at the end of January or July, usually not before the 28th day of the month. It is very important to mention that Cybermetrics Lab follows its general rule not to discuss any presented result or provide unprocessed data with which a specific ranking was performed [58].

4. Webometrics ranking system: advantages and disadvantages

Like other ranking systems, Webometrics ranking system has a range of advantages and disadvantages. Differently from other systems of ranking of scientists and universities, one can say that webometrics is a "global" ranking system. Why global? Most of the ranking systems include only several hundreds or thousands of the best universities, such as Shanghai list, while Webometrics includes most of the universities of the world, i.e., currently 28,000 scientific institutions from all over the world [60]. This list also enables ranking of scientific institutions, institutes, and individual members of a university, which can entice competitive spirit among individual members of a university. Why is this important? An extremely small number of universities of the world satisfy the Shanghai list criterium. However, this does not mean that there are no other universities of good quality besides those which are ranked as well as scientists working at those universities all over the world. It is easy to conclude that the universities from the Shanghai list and similar lists mainly originate from countries from well-developed economics and well-ordered educational systems, developed democracies, and high degrees of autonomies of their universities. Higher education systems of developed economies follow up the needs of the labor market and technology progress, and the quality of educational institutions is institutionally maintained due to strict accreditation criteria prescribed by authorized organs and ministries in every state. In developing countries and in poorly developed economies, there are great problems regarding an objective assessment and ranking of quality of institutions of higher education due to:

- Poor or no applying of international criteria [61, 62]
- Involvement of politics into institutions of higher education [61, 62]
- Devaluation of diplomas and criteria through institutions which do not fulfill requirements and criteria prescribed by law [61, 62]
- An extremely low percentage of scientific production of relevant publications indexed in the leading databases

In such circumstances, Webometrics ranking system actually represents a system of neutral international evaluation of quality of scientific institutions and scientists at all institutions not included into the Shanghai list. It is important to underline that there are not any significant deviations in the placing of the first 100 ranked universities on the Shanghai list and on the Webometrics list. Namely, the Webometrics list, through the four of its criteria (**Table 2**) [60], evaluates situations at the universities all over the world and positions them on its lists assessing every of the four criteria individually. This ranking procedure cannot be affected by any university, ministry, or state trying to improve its institution's ranking position. In most of the low-developed or non-developed countries, there is not any adequate system to control and follow up the success of reforms or define weaknesses and evaluate destructiveness of the involvement of policy into activities of institutions of higher education. This is one of the great advantages of Webometrics because it actually represents a very simple international tool for quality control of higher education institutions and enables competition among higher education institutions all over the world. In such process, it is clearly visible through the ranking system which of the four ranking parameters (presence, visibility, transparency, excellence) an institution progresses or stagnates. This enables development of a strategy for improvement of quality of scientific institutions, particularly in the weakest segments being evaluated. An extremely good point of Webometrics is that it performs ranking of institutions within states, within regions, or within the whole world [63]. In total, a university can be better positioned in some country, but it does not simultaneously mean that it is better than others by all of the four ranking parameters.

According to the last Webometrics list for Bosnia and Herzegovina [64] (January 2019, Edition 2019.1.2.), the University of Banja Luka is positioned second in Bosnia and Herzegovina, but in "presence rank" category, the International University of Sarajevo (which, in total, takes only the fourth position in Bosnia and Herzegovina) is ranked better than the University of Banja Luka (**Figure 1**).

How important having an international ranking list as a corrective showing and assessing situation at higher education institutions in developing countries may be analyzed on the example of universities of Bosnia and Herzegovina. Bosnia and Herzegovina is composed of two entities (the Federation of Bosnia and Herzegovina and the Republic of Srpska), and the Federation of Bosnia and Herzegovina is administratively divided into ten cantons. At the level of the state, there is the Framework Law on Higher Education in Bosnia and Herzegovina, while at the level of entities and cantons, there are educational policies being implemented according to the laws of entities and cantons. There are 8 public and 35 private universities and faculties in Bosnia and Herzegovina which are ranked by the Webometrics list from January 2019 (January 2019, Edition 2019.1.2.) [64], which is an extremely great number for the country with about 3.5 million of inhabitants. Work permits and work control of these higher education institutions, without clear international criteria, are issued and implemented by cantonal ministries of education with laws differing from canton to canton. Cantonal laws often are not in compliance with the Framework Law on Higher Education in Bosnia and Herzegovina ("Official Gazette of Bosnia and Herzegovina" no. 59/07 and 59/09, hereinafter: the Framework Law), and very often they are subjects of dispute before the Constitutional Court of Bosnia and Herzegovina (rating of constitutionality: U-19/16, U-22/18) [65, 66]. Cantonal laws are often changed for the purpose of involvement of politics into the universities in order to weaken and cancel their autonomy which is guaranteed by the Framework Law on Higher Education in Bosnia and Herzegovina. In such conditions, the only measure and objective evaluation is the Webometrics list. Namely, the University of Tuzla has been progressing on the Webometrics list over the years

Bosnia and Herzegovina

ranking	World Rank	University	Det.	Presence Rank*	Impact Rank*	Openness Rank*	Excellence Rank*
1	1785	University of Sarajevo / Univerzitet u Sarajevu		560	2231	1419	2334
2	3416	University of Banja Luka / Univerzitet u Banjoj Luci / Универзитет у Бањој Луци		1198	7284	3848	3414
3	3619	International BURCH University Sarajevo		741	6427	4049	3925
4	3671	International University of Sarajevo		660	7245	4129	3816
5	3795	University of Tuzla / Univerzitet u Tuzli		2347	7938	3610	3816
6	4840	University of Zenica / Univerzitet u Zenici		2631	8413	6451	4666
7	5027	University of Mostar / Sveučilište u Mostaru		1302	13403	4257	4269
8	5694	Sarajevo School of Science & Technology		17771	13223	3826	4566
9	6041	European University Brčko / Evropski Univerzitet		11223	4188	7607	6033
10	6635	Evropski Univerzitet Kallos Tuzla		12943	4225	9676	6033
11	6915	University of East Sarajevo / Univerzitet u Istocnom Sarajevu / Универзитет у Источном Сарајеву		1396	20114	5109	4269
12	9830	International University of Travnik / Internacionalni Univerzitet Travnik		4995	7225	11401	6033
13	11257	University Dzemal Bijedic Mostar / Univerzitet Džemal Bijedic Mostar		4671	11854	9938	6033

Figure 1.
The Webometrics list for Bosnia and Herzegovina with all parameters (January 2019, Edition 2019.1.2.) [64].

(after implementation of a set of measures by a quality team), and in June 2016, it took the 3186th position on the list, which was the best position of this university in the history (**Figure 2**). Immediately after this event, the Law on Higher Education in Tuzla Canton was changed, and in a day the management of the university was replaced, the Senate was dissolved, and receivership with temporary organs under political patronage was imposed. Although it is difficult to find such case in developed economies, or anywhere in the world, the key issue is how to measure the effect of such measure.

In circumstances where there is not any adequate reaction of state institutions (Agency for Higher Education, parliamentary committees for education, state Ministry for Civil Affairs) to such situation because everything is politically controlled and the Constitutional Court is declared authorized for interpretation of compliance of the Cantonal Law on Higher Education with the Framework Law on Higher Education in Bosnia and Herzegovina (U-19/16) [65], an independent international factor unaffected by politics, i.e., Webometrics, is necessary. Although such measure was allegedly implemented to improve quality and position of the University of Tuzla, the Webometrics list soon showed all the effects of this measure. The position of the University of Tuzla on the Webometrics list was becoming weaker and weaker over the years, and in January 2019, it ended on the 3795th [64] place (**Figure 2**) and experienced the fall for 609 positions or 19.11%. The university which in July 2016 (**Figure 2**) took the second position in Bosnia and Herzegovina by quality took the 5th place. One more advantage of Webometrics is ranking of four segments, which provides an insight into segments where the university became weaker and into those where it became stronger. The mentioned indicators show fall of quality in almost all of the ranked segments, and it imposes the conclusion that cancelation of autonomy, involvement of politics into the university, and compulsory administration cause weakening of the quality of the university. Similar processes and measures were implemented at the University of Bihać, which

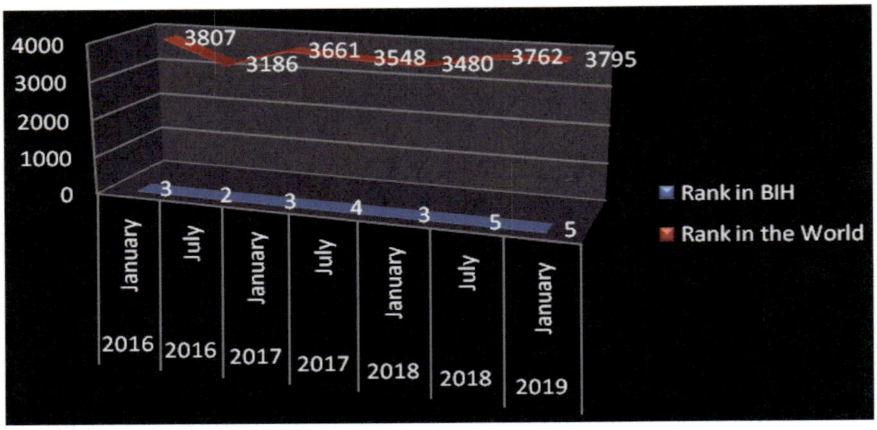

Figure 2.
Position of the University of Tuzla in the world and in Bosnia and Herzegovina according to the Webometrics list for the period from January 2016 to January 2019.

resulted in its taking 11,546th position according to the list from January 2019 [64], and it would be very hard to improve its position significantly. This resulted in a significant decrease of the number of enrolled students, in the decrease of competitiveness, and in the struggle for huge international projects and low percentage of scientific production in the leading index bases of the world. An obvious decline of publishing and quoting of works is confirmed by the criterium of excellence by which the University of Tuzla takes the 4th place in Bosnia and Herzegovina [64], with a condition that the mentioned parameters probably are not correct which is a consequence of Google Scholar and webometrics itself. Although it measures the researching productivity on the basis of the presence on the web, the mentioned ranking system depends on categories related to publishing and quoting of scientific works (of excellence (SCImago) and transparency (Google Scholar)) [60]. These two parameters bring 45% out of the total score in ranking of a university. Over the years there has been a notable tendency of increase of the weight of these two parameters in Webometrics ranking system. Here we see first the disadvantages of Webometrics ranking system. Webometrics uses GS for transparency criterium, which enables creation of a profile of a scientist with verification of an address from a scientific institution.

Google Scholar is a system in which the academic community has been very interested [67], and it has been used by a great number of universities and research institutions both for ranking of institutions and ranking of academic personnel [68–72]. The system is very good; it is automatized in the way that a computer program performs the main role in the whole process, from data collection to data processing. Like any other system, this one is not perfect, and it has some critical omissions which are mostly related to ascribing a quotation from a scientific paper to some authors to whom it does not belong.

GS system has several possibilities to ascribe articles to their authors. The first possibility is automatic. Computer system collects information about published scientific publications on the web, with all auxiliary elements of the paper which besides the title of the work include names of the authors, keywords, and a brief description of the paper. According to these data, GS system browses its basis of user profiles and proposes to a potential author found in its database of publications, which contains a name of a potential author, to ascribe the found article to his/her profile. On the basis of available data, GS system "assumes" that the user is the author of the publication found, which does not have to be true. This often causes situations where papers and quotes on certain profiles are not true. Of course, an author has to have his/her profile on GS system.

Another possibility is manual addition of a publication with all of its auxiliary meta-information. By this approach, GS system enables a user who has a profile on the system to enter data about his/her paper manually: a title of the paper, a list of all authors, a name of a publisher, a title of a journal or a conference, a year of publication, etc. There is not any mechanism to check authenticity of an author, i.e., if a person is the author or a co-author of the paper. The only good point of this approach, bearing in mind manipulation of quotes in the concerned publication, is that all quotes related to the paper concerned would not unconditionally be ascribed to the user of a profile, i.e., to the "author" who adds the paper to his/her profile. A possible explanation for this situation may be in the fact that there is not any possibility to acquire all quotes of a paper at once since it is done automatically by web crawler computers which have their time scheme of performance of tasks.

The third possibility is to add publications manually but not data. One browses the database of GS system and finds a desired publication and ascribes it to the user profile. This differs from the previous approach by the fact that the work concerned was already indexed in GS system and all necessary data (which besides the main data contain data about all quotes related to the publication) were ascribed to it. In this case, if a publication having a certain number of quotes has already been ascribed to an author who is its real author and if a user manually adds the publication to his/her profile, then all existing quotes of the publication concerned would be ascribed to his/her profile regardless of the fact that he/she is not the real author or co-author of the publication. According to our best knowledge, currently there is not any mechanism to heck credibility of an author—if a person really is the author of the co-author of the concerned publication. This is one of the great disadvantages of the current version of GS system regarding manual ascription of publications to users' profiles.

Since we believe that the last mentioned situation represents a serious omission in GS system, we tested the concerned situation with two articles. One publication which we added to a profile of a user (with No = 47 quotes) who is not the author of the publication (one of the authors of this article) had a significant number of quotes (No = 388), while the other one did not (No = 20). Two publications with different numbers of quotes were added in order to check if it was really practically possible to add a publication with any number of quotes. We made a screenshot before adding the concerned publications to the profile of a user who was not the author of any of the articles (**Figure 3**) and after the publications were added (**Figure 4**). These two illustrations clearly show that after the concerned publications were added, the number of quotes of "new author" increased significantly proportionally to the number of quotes ascribed to the source publication. GS system did not, at any time, report that the "new author " actually was not the author of the concerned publications.

This represents significant omission in Google Scholar system, which opens possibilities for new ways of manipulation in all systems of ranking, of universities, and of researchers themselves, which use this system as a part of some other systems for various types of ranking. Some authors had already been pointing to manipulations with quotes in academic researches [73], but this is the case of manipulation of GS system [74, 75].

Where does this omission become very "disputable?" Namely, examining profiles of scientists from the University of Tuzla, one defined that even 30% of profiles out of the first ten ranked contain papers of which they are not authors or co-authors. Those are profiles taken into consideration in ranking of parameters on the list from January 2019. It is significant to mention that even 446 quotes

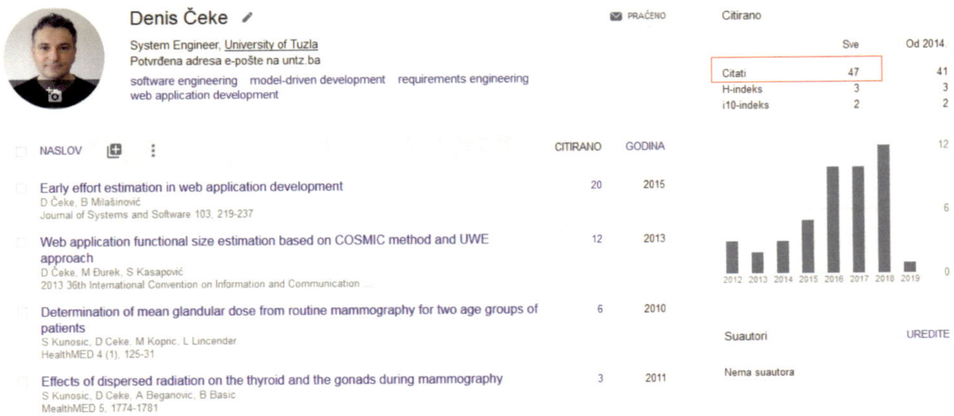

Figure 3.
Author's profile on GS with an accurate number of quotes.

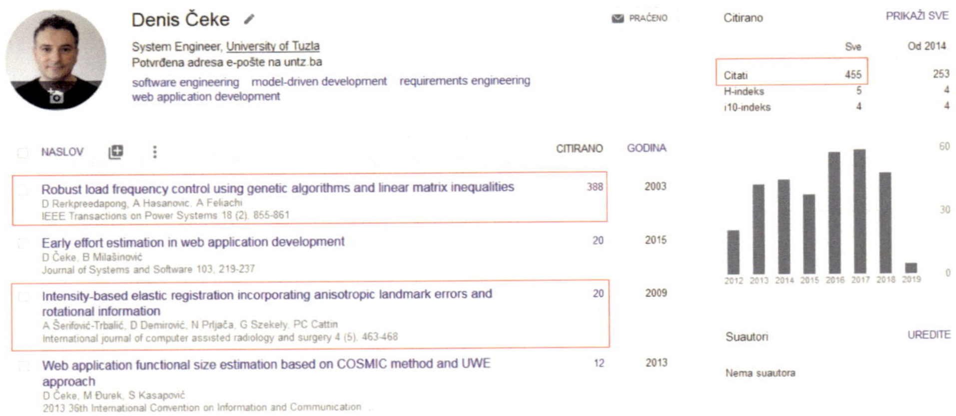

Figure 4.
Author's profile on GS after adding two papers with belonging quotes.

which do not belong were ascribed to the mentioned profiles [76]. This data becomes extremely significant if we consider the fact that only 8 scientists from the University of Tuzla have more than 400 quotes (the real number is even less when one takes out nonexisting quotes and scientists who do not work at the University of Tuzla anymore). Analyzing the following 10 profiles of scientists (by order of 11–20), we found 186 more non-belonging quotes [76]. This becomes a greater problem if we bear in mind that most of those "added" works were published in journals of extremely good quality [76], so the quotes have been distributed over the years which affects the parameters of ranking of the university even more. If we know that the first ten ranked profiles are taken into consideration in ranking, we have to ask ourselves if those are really the best ranked scientists and if the position of the university on the Webometrics list is dully calculated [76]. A checkup may easily show that the order, the number of quotes, and the index are not correct, which leads us to a process of incorrect ranking of profiles and incorrect evaluation of the Webometrics list. Knowing the evaluation system on which webometrics functions, it is easy to conclude that adding highly quoted papers from prestigious publications can significantly improve the position of a university. This is also extremely important for ranking of scientists because many universities in the world do not have any access to WOS, and it is very easy for all to use GS ranking lists to measure quality of scientists and a degree of their being quoted. These lists

DOI: http://dx.doi.org/10.5772/intechopen.87207

should be reviewed in order to obtain a realistic picture in ranking of scientists in institutions and by states as an adequate hierarchy of universities. The example from our experiment can easily show that h-index has changed significantly. By adding only two papers, it increased from 3 to even 5, and i-index increased from 2 to 4 (**Figures 3** and **4**). Since the mentioned omissions were found at many other universities as well, we believe that changes in the ranking order of universities and scientists would be very significant. Authors on profiles often are not aware that those are not their works because they update their profiles automatically. Many of them do not pay great attention to it, while a great number of scientists do not have a great knowledge about ranking systems. Another disadvantage of this system is retention of scientists' profiles, although they are engaged by another institution. This means that their profiles are retained after cessation of their engagements. Movements of scientists in the system of scientific institutions and going from one institution to another for the purpose of increasing quality of individual institutions are also a process which should be followed up by GS. To solve this problem, one needs to design a system which would obligate scientific institutions to update data in time and to ask for removal of profiles of those scientists who are not engaged anymore (i.e., the profiles should be adjusted to the new institution). Gaining benefits for quotes on profiles of retired scientists and of those who passed away by institutions is not fair. We found such omission at our university where even 2 out of the first 12 scientists left the University of Tuzla, having together over 1300 citations and being involved in the process of ranking of the university [76]. This omission may not be ascribed only to GS, but one needs to design a system of annual verification of profiles for which scientific institution would be in charge. On the other hand, there are scientists who are not ranked within the frame of an institution due to wrong entries of affiliation and do not contribute to the reputation of a university although they have a great number of quotes. Although Webometrics in its rules hinted at a possibility of sanctioning institutions for double profiles and ascribing papers to wrong authors [60], we noticed that the mentioned sanction has not been implemented, and we saw such cases at several universities in Bosnia and Herzegovina. There is a simple way to solve the mentioned manipulations and omissions. One of the ways is introduction of *Z* score system [77–79] into Webometrics ranking system. Namely, this system would check authorship, i.e., it would be impossible that a system or a man adds a paper to a scientist's profile if he/she is not its author. For the purpose of further increase of quality of ranking related to publications, one could think about introduction of a certain percentage of ranking on the basis of publications indexed in the best databases in WOS through this system. Authors would also be ranked by the volume of work, i.e., *Z* score would perform ranking of scientist on the basis of a type of authorship (first author, corresponding author, other authors), number of authors of a paper, quality of a journal, and a number of quotes. Should this process be too demanding in the first phase, a process of filtration of profiles and removal of double profiles, non-belonging papers, and other omissions could be performed in the first phase.

5. Conclusion

As a global ranking system, webometrics represents an important step in the assessment of scientific institutions and scientists. It is very important, especially in countries which do not implement international standards and criteria through their institutional educational system. Through its main four parameters, the system entices healthy competition among scientific institutions and scientists. Along with all of the advantages, the system, like any other system, has some disadvantages, mostly in the domain of ranking of scientists and therefore of institutions through valorization of publications and quotes. Manipulations with a number of quotes and calculation of h-index and i-index can be removed with the application of new systems for measuring, such as Z score, or by introduction of new algorithms for recognition and prevention of these disadvantages.

Author details

Suad Kunosić[1*], Denis Čeke[2] and Enver Zerem[3]

1 Department of Physics, Faculty of Natural Sciences and Mathematics, University of Tuzla, Tuzla, Bosnia and Herzegovina

2 University of Tuzla, Tuzla, Bosnia and Herzegovina

3 Department of Medical Sciences, Academy of Sciences and Arts of Bosnia and Herzegovina, University Džemal Bijedić Mostar, Bosnia and Herzegovina

*Address all correspondence to: suad.kunosic@untz.ba

References

[1] Björneborn L, Ingwersen P. Toward a basic framework for webometrics. Journal of the American Society for Information Science and Technology. 2004;**55**:1216-1227. DOI: 10.1002/asi.20077

[2] Thelwall M. A history of webometrics. Bulletin of the American Society for Information Science and Technology. 2012;**38**:18-23. DOI: 10.1002/bult.2012.1720380606

[3] Almind TC, Ingwersen P. Informetric analyses on the world wide web: Methodological approaches to 'webometrics'. Journal of Documentation. 1997;**53**:404-426. DOI: 10.1108/EUM0000000007205

[4] Björneborn L, Ingwersen P. Perspective of webometrics. Scientometrics. 2001;**50**:65-82. DOI: 10.1023/A:1005642218907

[5] Thelwall M. Introduction to Webometrics: Quantitative web research for the social sciences. Synthesis Lectures on Information Concepts, Retrieval, and Services. 2009;**1**:1-116. DOI: 10.2200/S00176ED1V01Y200903ICR004

[6] Ingwersen P. The calculation of web impact factors. Journal of Documentation. 1998;**54**:236-243. DOI: 10.1108/EUM0000000007167

[7] Åström F. Changes in the LIS research front: Time-sliced cocitation analyses of LIS journal articles, 1990-2004. Journal of the American Society for Information Science and Technology. 2007;**58**:947-957. DOI: 10.1002/asi.20567

[8] Zhao. Information science during the first decade of the web: An enriched author cocitation analysis. Journal of the American Society for Information Science and Technology. Wiley Online Library n.d. 2008. Available from: https://onlinelibrary.wiley.com/doi/full/10.1002/asi.20799 [Accessed: January 30, 2019]

[9] Thelwall M. Extracting macroscopic information from web links. Journal of the American Society for Information Science and Technology. 2001;**52**:1157-1168. DOI: 10.1002/asi.1182

[10] Bar-Ilan J. The use of web search engines in information science research. Annual Review of Information Science and Technology. 2004;**38**:231-288. DOI: 10.1002/aris.1440380106

[11] Aguillo IF, Granadino B, Ortega JL, Prieto JA. Scientific research activity and communication measured with cybermetrics indicators. Journal of the American Society for Information Science and Technology. 2006;**57**:1296-1302. DOI: 10.1002/asi.20433

[12] Thelwall M. Webometrics: Emergent or doomed? n.d. Available from: http://www.informationr.net/ir/15-4/colis713.html [Accessed: January 28, 2019]

[13] Li X, Thelwall M, Musgrove P, Wilkinson D. The relationship between the WIFs or inlinks of computer science departments in UK and their RAE ratings or research productivities in 2001. Scientometrics. 2003;**57**:239-255. DOI: 10.1023/A:1024189702463

[14] Thelwall M, Stuart D. The use of Webometrics for the analysis of knowledge flows within the European research area. Framework Service Contract for Expert Support with the Production and Analy-Sis of R&D Policy Indicators. 2009. Available from: http://ec.europa.eu/invest-in-research/pdf/download_en/spa6_final_report.pdf [Accessed: January 28, 2019]

[15] Thelwall M. Bibliometrics to webometrics. Journal of Information

Science. 2008;**34**:605-621. DOI: 10.1177/0165551507087238

[16] Thomas O, Willett P. Webometric analysis of departments of librarianship and information science. Journal of Information Science. 2000;**26**:421-428. DOI: 10.1177/016555150002600605

[17] Barjak F, Thelwall M. A statistical analysis of the web presences of European life sciences research teams. Journal of the American Society for Information Science and Technology. 2008;**59**:628-643. DOI: 10.1002/asi.20776

[18] Barjak F, Li X, Thelwall M. Which factors explain the web impact of scientists' personal homepages? Journal of the American Society for Information Science and Technology. 2007;**58**:200-211. DOI: 10.1002/asi.20476

[19] Thelwall M, Vaughan L, Björneborn L. Webometrics. Annual Review of Information Science and Technology. 2005;**39**:81-135. DOI: 10.1002/aris.1440390110

[20] Yang B, Qin J. Data collection system for link analysis. In: Pichappan P, Abraham A, editors. Third IEEE International Conference on Digital Information Management (ICDIM), November 13-16, 2008, London, UK, Proceedings. IEEE. 2008. pp. 247-252. DOI: 10.1109/ICDIM.2008.4746781

[21] SocSciBot: Link crawler for the social sciences. n.d. Available from: http://socscibot.wlv.ac.uk/ [Accessed: January 29, 2019]

[22] Webometric Analyst: Altmetrics, web citation analysis, alternative indicators, link analysis, social web. n.d. Available from: http://lexiurl.wlv.ac.uk/ [Accessed: January 29, 2019]

[23] Thelwall M, Sud P. Webometric research with the Bing search API 2.0. Journal of Informetrics. 2012;**6**:44-52. DOI: 10.1016/j.joi.2011.10.002

[24] Sherman C, Price G, Sullivan D. The Invisible Web: Uncovering Information Sources Search Engines Can't See. Information Today, Inc./CyberAge Books; 2001

[25] Gomes B, Smith BT. Detecting query-specific duplicate documents. US6615209B12003

[26] Thelwall M. Extracting accurate and complete results from search engines: Case study windows live. Journal of the American Society for Information Science and Technology. 2008;**59**:38-50. DOI: 10.1002/asi.20704

[27] Vaughan L, Thelwall M. Search engine coverage bias: Evidence and possible causes. Information Processing and Management. 2004;**40**:693-707. DOI: 10.1016/S0306-4573(03)00063-3

[28] Thelwall M. Quantitative comparisons of search engine results. Journal of the American Society for Information Science and Technology. 2008;**59**:1702-1710. DOI: 10.1002/asi.20834

[29] LexiURL Searcher Classic. n.d. Available from: http://lexiurl.wlv.ac.uk/searcher/usingLexiURLSearcherClassic.html [Accessed: January 30, 2019]

[30] Program Package Pajek/PajekXXL n.d. Available from: http://mrvar.fdv.uni-lj.si/pajek/ [Accessed: January 29, 2019]

[31] UCINET Software n.d. Available from: https://sites.google.com/site/ucinetsoftware/home [Accessed: January 29, 2019]

[32] Borgatti S. NetDraw 2002. Available from: https://sites.google.com/site/netdrawsoftware/home [Accessed: January 29, 2019]

[33] Cooper K. Keyword research, competitor analysis, & website ranking | Alexa. AlexaCom n.d. Available from: https://www.alexa.com/ [Accessed: January 29, 2019]

[34] Alexa Internet. Firefox Browser Extension Download. n.d. Available from: https://www.alexa.com/toolbar [Accessed: January 29, 2019]

[35] WHOIS Search, Domain Name, Website, and IP Tools—Who.is n.d. Available from: https://who.is/ [Accessed: January 29, 2019]

[36] SEO Tools—Search Engine Optimization Tools. n.d. Available from: https://www.webconfs.com/ [Accessed: January 29, 2019]

[37] Majestic®: Marketing Search Engine and SEO Backlink Checker n.d. Available from: https://majestic.com/ [Accessed: January 29, 2019]

[38] The ultimate SEO Research Tool | Searchmetrics Essentials. Searchmetrics 2016. https://www.searchmetrics.com/essentials/ [Accessed: January 29, 2019]

[39] Google PageRank Checker—Check Google page rank instantly n.d. Available from: https://www.prchecker.info/check_page_rank.php [Accessed: January 29, 2019]

[40] Ahrefs Team. n.d. Available from: https://ahrefs.com/about [Accessed: January 29, 2019]

[41] Site Explorer by Ahrefs: Competitive Analysis Tool For SEO. n.d. Available from: https://ahrefs.com/site-explorer [Accessed: January 29, 2019]

[42] Content Explorer by Ahrefs: Get Content Ideas on Any Topic. n.d. Available from: https://ahrefs.com/content-explorer [Accessed: January 29, 2019]

[43] Keywords Explorer by Ahrefs: A Potent Keyword Tool. n.d. Available from: https://ahrefs.com/keywords-explorer [Accessed: January 30, 2019]

[44] Rank Tracker by Ahrefs: Check & Track Keyword Rankings. n.d. Available from: https://ahrefs.com/rank-tracker [Accessed: January 29, 2019]

[45] SEO Site Audit tool by Ahrefs. n.d. Available from: https://ahrefs.com/site-audit [Accessed: January 29, 2019]

[46] Definition of RANKING n.d. Available from: https://www.merriam-webster.com/dictionary/ranking [Accessed: January 29, 2019]

[47] Vernon MM, Balas EA, Momani S. Are university rankings useful to improve research? A systematic review. PLoS One. 2018;**13**:e0193762. DOI: 10.1371/journal.pone.0193762

[48] Aguillo IF, Bar-Ilan J, Levene M, Ortega JL. Comparing university rankings. Scientometrics. 2010;**85**: 243-256. DOI: 10.1007/s11192-010-0190-z

[49] Google. n.d. Available from: https://www.google.com/ [Accessed: January 30, 2019]

[50] Consejo Superior de Investigaciones Científicas (CSIC). csic.es. n.d. Available from: http://www.csic.es/ [Accessed: January 29, 2019]

[51] Aguillo IF, Ortega JL, Fernández M. Webometric ranking of world universities: Introduction, methodology, and future developments. Higher Education in Europe. 2008;**33**:233-244. DOI: 10.1080/03797720802254031

[52] ARWU World University Rankings 2018 | Academic Ranking of World Universities n.d. Available from: http://www.shanghairanking.com/ [Accessed: January 29, 2019]

[53] Wouters P, Reddy C, Aguillo I. On the visibility of information on the web:

An exploratory experimental approach. Research Evaluation. 2006;**15**:107-115. DOI: 10.3152/147154406781775931

[54] Web indicators: A new generation of S&T indicators › KNAW Research Portal. n.d. Available from: https://pure.knaw.nl/portal/en/publications/webindicators-a-new-generation-of-st-indicators(3a0f58a7-14dc-47c5-9123-ee3c8b0983d5)/export.html [Accessed: January 29, 2019]

[55] Bar-Ilan J. Expectations Versus Reality—Search Engine Features Needed for Web Research at Mid 2005; 2005

[56] Link Analysis: An Information Science Approach. Vol. 04. Emerald Group Publishing Limited; 2004. pp. 265-269. DOI: 10.1108/S1876-0562(2004)0000004028

[57] Cothey V. Web-crawling reliability. Journal of the American Society for Information Science and Technology. 2004;**55**:1228-1238. DOI: 10.1002/asi.20078

[58] Ranking Web of Universities: More than 28000 institutions ranked. Updated every January and July: Webometrics, Bibliometrics, Altmetrics. n.d. Available from: http://www.webometrics.info/en [Accessed: January 29, 2019]

[59] Zitt M, Filliatreau G. Big Is (Made) Beautiful some Comments about the Shanghai Ranking of World-Class Universities. 2007. pp. 141-160

[60] Methodology. Ranking Web of Universities: More than 28000 institutions ranked. n.d. Available from: http://www.webometrics.info/en/Methodology [Accessed: January 29, 2019]

[61] Zerem E. Right criteria for academia in Bosnia and Herzegovina. The Lancet. 2013;**382**(9887):128

[62] Zerem E. Academic community in a developing country: Bosnian realities. Medicinski Glasnik (Zenica). 2014;**11**(2):248-251

[63] Ranking Web of Universities: Ranking by Areas. Available from: http://www.webometrics.info/en/node/18 [Accessed: April 12, 2019]

[64] Ranking Web of Universities: Bosnia and Herzegovina. Available from: http://www.webometrics.info/en/Europe/Bosnia%20and%20Herzegovina%20 [Accessed: April 12, 2019]

[65] Constitutional Court of Bosnia and Herzegovina: Decisions. Available from: http://www.ustavnisud.ba/dokumenti/_bs/U-19-16-1067890.pdf [Accessed: April 12, 2019]

[66] Constitutional Court of Bosnia and Herzegovina: The Case in the Procesc. Available from: http://www.ccbh.ba/odluke/#

[67] Butler D. Computing giants launch free science metrics. Nature. 2011;**476**(7358):18-18

[68] Jacso P. Deflated, inflated and phantom citation counts. Online Information Review. 2006;**30**(3):297-309. [Accessed: April 12, 2019]

[69] Jacsó P. The plausibility of computing the h-index of scholarly productivity and impact using reference-enhanced databases. Online Information Review. 2008;**32**(2):266-283

[70] Jacsó P. Metadata mega mess in Google Scholar. Online Information Review. 2010;**34**(1):175-191

[71] Jacsó P. Calculating the h-index and other bibliometric and scientometric indicators from Google Scholar with the publish or perish software. Online Information Review. 2009;**33**(6):1189-1200

[72] Aguillo IF. Is Google Scholar useful for bibliometrics? A webometric analysis. Scientometrics. 2012;**91**(2):343-351

[73] Fong EA, Wilhite AW. Authorship and citation manipulation in academic research. PLoS One. 2017;**12**(12):e0187394

[74] Lopez-Cozar ED, Robinson-Garcia N, Torres-Salinas D. Manipulating Google Scholar citations and Google Scholar metrics: Simple, easy and tempting. In: EC3 Working Papers 6. 2012

[75] Delgado-López-Cózar E, Cabezas-Clavijo Á. Google Scholar Metrics: An unreliable tool for assessing scientific journals. El Profesional de la información. 2012;**21**(4):1386-6710

[76] Google Scholar: Profiles University of Tuzla. Available from: https://scholar.google.hr/citations?view_op=view_org&hl=hr&org=13570989470062067060 [Accessed: April 7, 2019]

[77] Zerem E. The ranking of scientists based on scientific publications assessment. Journal of Biomedical Informatics. 2017;**75**:107-109

[78] Zerem E. The ranking of scientists. Journal of Biomedical Informatics. 2018;**79**:147

[79] Zerem E, Kunosić S. The ranking of scientists: Computational calculation of Z-score. Journal of Biomedical Informatics. 2018;**81**:133

Section 2

Bibliometrics and Its Applications

Chapter 3

Bibliometric Method for Mapping the State-of-the-Art and Identifying Research Gaps and Trends in Literature: An Essential Instrument to Support the Development of Scientific Projects

Otávio José de Oliveira, Fabio Francisco da Silva, Fernando Juliani, Luis César Ferreira Motta Barbosa and Thaís Vieira Nunhes

Abstract

Bibliometric analysis is an indispensable statistic tool to map the state of the art in a given area of scientific knowledge and identify essential information for various purposes, such as prospecting research opportunities and substantiating scientific researches. Therefore, the objective of this chapter is to present a method of bibliometric analysis for mapping the state of the art and identifying gaps and trends of research. The method encompasses instruments to identify and analyze the scientific performance of articles, authors, institutions, countries, and journals based on the number of citations, to reveal the trends of the field studied through the analysis of keywords, and to identify and cluster scientific gaps from most recent publications. This method enables to expand in a scientific way the boundaries of science by investigating and identifying relevant and avant-garde research topics. It is an essential element that provides researchers means to identify and support paths towards the development of scientific projects.

Keywords: bibliometric method, bibliometric analysis, research gaps, trends in literature, scientific projects

1. Introduction

The scenario of intense competitiveness is a reality that has led many countries to increasingly invest in their scientific and technological development, which is an essential pillar for the construction of a sustainable economy [1].

One of the consequences of this development is the large volume of scientific articles published daily in international databases for the dissemination and sharing of contributions and advances resulting from academic research of different groups of researchers from various universities and countries [1, 2].

In light of this, the importance of bibliometrics is worth noting, which is a method for measuring, monitoring, and studying scientific outputs [3, 4]. Bibliometrics enables the mapping and expansion of knowledge on a particular area of research, evidencing connections between the main publications, authors, institutions, themes, and other characteristics of the field under study [3, 5].

An important application of bibliometric methods is its use as a tool for research evaluation [2, 4]. Outstanding papers in bibliometric studies are considered as reliable and relevant sources of results and are often used to justify decisions on research policies, funds, job offers, and promotions and also to direct and support research projects on the basis of what is most relevant in the scientific literature [2, 6].

The evolution of knowledge is something that occurs all the time, and the novelty of the researchers' proposals is the basic premise for the development of scientific research with great scientific and applied contributions. Therefore, the analysis of the state of the art of the field studied is an indispensable step to choose a no table research problem, since it can reveal gaps that need to be filled in the literature and important studies to underpin the researchers' proposals [6].

In this sense, it is important to emphasize that research funding bodies have increasingly required evidence that the research they support has potential to impact society with innovations, advances, etc. [2, 4, 7, 8].

Bibliometric methods involve the use of several tools that can help researchers to identify a relevant and current research problem, thus making clear the potential impact of the research in case of it being developed [4, 6].

Information technology (IT) tools can be used to assist the process of searching for relevant scientific contents, collecting scientific data, and summarizing the results obtained. These tools may be extremely important in clarifying the direction of a particular field of study and what advances and developments this may still present [4, 6].

Bibliometric indicators, if properly analyzed, can give more consistence to the research project, since they use statistics from different bibliographic databases that differ in terms of scope, data volume, and coverage [4].

Thus, the researcher who develops the research project based on bibliometric analysis has the possibility of presenting the objectives and methods of his work clearly and concisely by illustrating which scientific gaps in the field will be filled with the development of its study.

Hence, the purpose of this chapter is to present a method of bibliometric analysis for mapping the state of the art and identifying gaps and trends of research in literature. Throughout the sections some important bibliometric tools and analysis to justify the development of research projects will be set out.

The proper use of the presented method allows the understanding of the gaps and research tendencies from the mapping of the state of the art of a field studied, being a path to be followed by researchers in the phase of elaboration of their research project in order to ensure that the studies present real scientific, applied, and social contributions.

2. Mining and analysis of bibliometric data

The application of this method is oriented to map the state of the art of a scientific theme through the characterization of bibliometric parameters. The bibliometric parameters used are those with greater availability in scientific research platforms. For this characteristic, the presented method has universal application in the different fields of knowledge, concerning the researcher to adapt it adequately to meet their demands of study.

Another relevant characteristic of the method is that it was primarily designed to be applied in the initial phase of the development of a new study. Through the mapping of the state of the art, the bibliometric analysis reveals to the researcher essential information to base his study. The application of bibliometric analysis in the initial phase of a study can ensure that relevant references of the literature were considered for the construction of the new research. In addition, the results of the bibliometric study sheds light on the gaps of the literature, what can substantiate the scientific demand and originality of the study proposed.

The expected results of conducting the bibliometric analysis proposed in this method can be achieved by performing the macro-steps presented in **Figure 1**.

After defining the field studied, with which it is advisable that the researcher has some affinity, the first challenge in the bibliometric study is the choice of the scientific research platform to be used.

The choice of the scientific research platform is one of the actions that has a significant impact on the bibliometric analysis and, therefore, must be well planned in order to obtain assertive results and avoid reworking. In practical terms, research

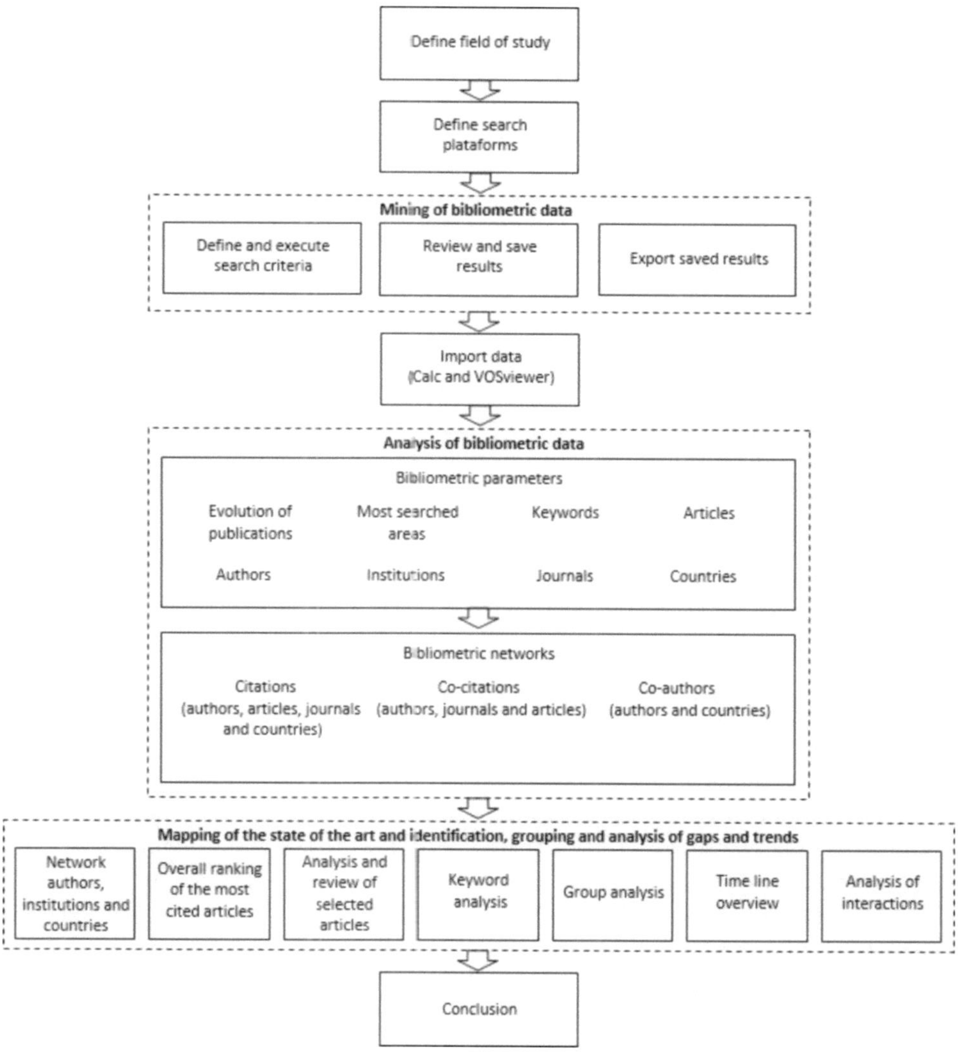

Figure 1.
Stages of the method for mapping the state of the art and identifying gaps and trends of research. Source: Prepared by the authors.

platforms present different tools for mining scientific data. Thus, the researcher should check what data can be extracted from each one of the platforms that best reflect the objectives of the study. This analysis is essential for the bibliometric study to meet the researcher's expectations and produce high-quality bibliometric studies.

Examples of scientific research platforms with robust databases and reasonable availability of search filters include Scopus (www.scopus.com) and Web of Science (WoS) (www.webofknowledge.com). These platforms provide access to thousands of scientific articles published by publishers such as Elsevier (www.sciencedirect.com), Emerald (www.emeraldinsight.com), Springer (www.springerlink.com), Wiley (www.wiley.com), and Taylor & Francis (www.tandfonline.com), among others. EBSCO (www.ebsco.com), Crossref (www.crossref.org), and Google Scholar (scholar.google.com) are other multidisciplinary platforms also used by researchers. In addition to these, there are extensive numbers of platforms specific to the different fields of knowledge.

The combination of one or more platforms for mining scientific data can result in more consistent bibliometric analysis. On the other hand, it will be more difficult to integrate information from platforms with different structures, and although there are computational tools that support the integration of this data, they still require great improvements.

Besides the structural differences between the platforms, there are also differences in the classification of the information adopted by each of them. For example, if the same search criteria were applied to different platforms, the results returned may not be the same. The variation in the number of articles is explained by the different search parameters adopted and also by the particular coverage of each platform.

The difference in the results generated by the platforms is approached in the works conducted by [9–12].

In this way, it concerns the researcher to identify the scientific research platforms that offer the largest collection of articles in their field of study. Throughout this chapter, the scientific platforms Scopus and WoS will be used as reference to operationalize the proposed method and integrate bibliometric data from these two platforms. The main reasons for using Scopus and WoS are the multidisciplinarity of these databases, once they cover a relevant and extensive collection of scientific publications and have available various tools for scientific data mining.

Scopus and WoS enable the extraction of essential data for conducting bibliometric analysis. From these data, it is possible to compare the performance of the literature according to each platform and corroborate, complement, or refute the results.

In addition, the integration of the scientific data provided by these platforms makes it possible to obtain more robust results for the bibliometric analysis. **Figure 2** presents the bibliometric data provided by the Scopus and WoS platforms.

Once the scientific platforms to be used have been defined, it is necessary to establish the search criteria of the articles. In order to obtain high-quality data mining, the search strategy should reliably reflect the research topic, the study objectives, and the limits of the research field. The main search criteria used in the bibliometric analysis are specific terms to the field of study, publication period, document type and language, and area of knowledge.

The specific terms of the field under study should express the subject, its synonyms, and different spellings. For example, the theme "Lean Six Sigma" is often represented by its synonym "Lean Sigma" or "Lean 6 Sigma". For more assertive results, it is recommended to use the Boolean expressions "AND" or "OR" to combine different expressions and increase the theme's specification, thus improving

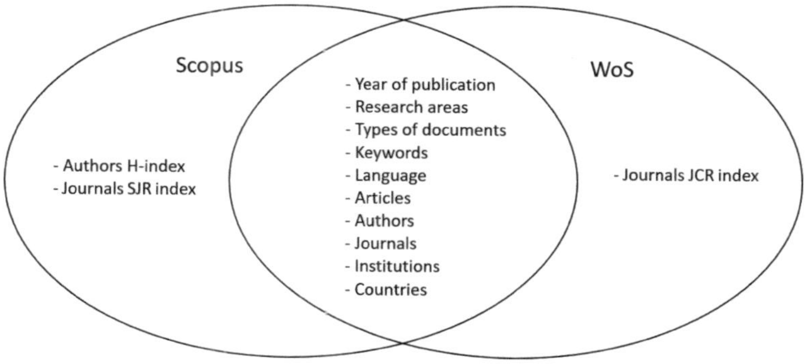

Figure 2.
Bibliometric data provided by scientific platforms Scopus and WoS. Source: Prepared by the authors.

the accuracy of the results returned. Specific terms of the field under study should be primarily sought in the titles, keywords, and summaries of the articles.

The filter of publication period should be defined according to the period in which the researcher wishes to perform the bibliometric analysis. For a complete map of the state of the art, it is suggested that all studies regardless of their year of publication be analyzed. However, when the fields of study have been investigated for many decades and the number of documents published is too high, it is advisable to limit the period analyzed because the subjects approached in the older papers were probably widely explored in the following ones. It should be highlighted that the analysis of gaps and trends for future research (discussed later in details) in general needs to be developed based on recent publications [13].

Among the different types of documents available on scientific platforms, articles and reviews published in journals are the most reliable source to review the literature, since they are peer-reviewed in their full version [14]. It is recommended not to include conference papers, notes, letters, books, book chapters, editorials, doctoral theses, master's dissertations, and nonscientific publications, except in cases where these types of documents are indispensable and relevant to the field studied. However, when it comes to the medical field of research, it is also necessary to take note of letters to the editor and case reports. The letters to the editor are documents that report important discussions for the development of medical research, being not so common in other scientific fields. Further, the case reports present the most recent findings or the limits to which modern medicine and technology are progressing and can be a channel for dissemination of best practices and solutions.

It is also suggested that only studies published in English be selected, since this is the universal language of the science.

The definition of the area of knowledge allows to limit the research to specific fields. However, if the researcher wishes to know the state of the art as a whole, it is recommended that the study be carried out considering all the areas of knowledge. If the amount of data found is extensive, the researcher may limit the investigation to only one area. **Table 1** presents an example of application of the search criteria to the study field on Lean Six Sigma.

The results that meet the previously established criteria are displayed, and the researcher must analyze the quality of the results. If the quality of the results is satisfactory, the researcher should save it in the user area of the search platform. The user area stores all the results obtained with the different applications of the search criteria. The articles saved in this user area will be the database used for conducting the bibliometric analysis. It is important to emphasize that before starting the data analysis, it is necessary to certify the search results to eliminate articles that do not belong to the field of study, but are included in the results.

	Inclusion criteria	Exclusion criteria
Database	Scopus and WoS	Others databases
Publication period	Up to 2017	Articles published in 2018
Document type	Articles and reviews	Conference papers, book chapters, books, notes, letters, editorials
Source type	Journals	Books, websites, conference proceedings, trade publications, doctoral thesis, masters dissertations
Subject area	Physical, life, social, health and humanities sciences	—
Language	English	Other languages
Source: Prepared by the authors.		

Table 1.
Example of application of the search criteria for the study field "Lean Six Sigma".

One of the errors in the mining of bibliometric data is the use of a word that has various meanings. For example, if you search for the term "Lean" many articles that belong to "Lean Manufacturing" search field will be selected. However, many articles that contain the word "Lean" to refer to a characteristic of the human body will also be returned.

For this reason, it is essential that the author be attentive to this analysis on the search results. It is recommended that the title of the article be analyzed first to verify its suitability for the purposes of the study. If there is any doubt after the examination of the title, it is necessary to read the article abstract. If the doubt persists, it is fundamental to analyze the full text to decide if the bibliometric data of this article will be exported to the software of bibliometric analysis.

Scientific platforms provide various bibliometric data, and among the most relevant to perform the bibliometric analysis are title of the article, authors, journal, year of publication, number of citations, institutions, countries, keywords, and bibliographic references. The choice of exporting all these data should be specified in the scientific platform itself, as shown in **Figures 3** and **4**.

Scientific platforms offer different options of file formats to be exported. The most suitable file formats for export are ".csv" and ".txt". These formats allow the bibliometric data to be analyzed in spreadsheets and/or bibliometric softwares.

Figure 3.
Selecting the data to be exported on the Scopus platform [15].

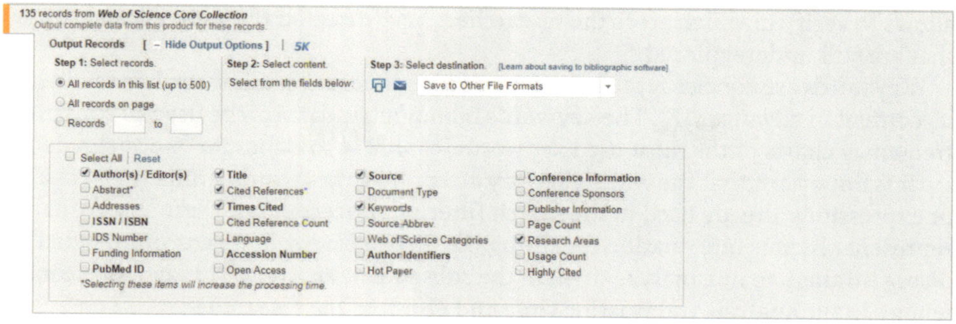

Figure 4.
Selecting the data to be exported on the WoS platform [16].

Bibliometric data	Bibliometric parameters
- Year of publication	- Evolution of publications
- Research areas	- Most searched areas
- Keywords	- Most used keywords
- Article title	- Most cited articles
- Authors	- Most cited authors
	- More productive authors
- Institutions	- Most cited institutions
	- More productive institutions
- Journals	- More productive journals
- Countries	- More productive countries

Source: Prepared by the authors.

Table 2.
Imported bibliometric data and bibliometric parameters generated.

In order to make bibliometric analysis more accessible to the scientific community, the presented method recommends the use of open source software such as Calc (LibreOffice), Sci2 Tool (CNS), and VOSviewer (Leiden University).

Calc is a spreadsheet, and its use covers two main purposes: to integrate bibliometric data from different scientific platforms and analyze them. The bibliometric data imported in the Calc spreadsheet and the respective bibliometric parameters generated are presented in **Table 2**.

Importing data into the spreadsheet will only occur when the files are exported in the correct format. For the Scopus platform, the file should be exported in the ".csv" format. On the WoS platform, the data should be exported in the ".txt" format ("tab-separated" option). With the data imported into separated worksheets, the researcher must organize them into a single worksheet and classify according to the title of the article. This activity will allow the identification of duplicate files, making possible their elimination.

The bibliometric parameter "evolution of publications" is based on the publication year of each article. To obtain this parameter, the spreadsheet must be operated to quantify the number of articles published per year. This parameter reveals the dynamics of the publications, whether the topic has been widely explored by researchers or if there is a reduction in the interest of the scientific community.

The bibliometric data of research areas are used to quantify which areas are the most researched ones. The information obtained by this bibliometric parameter allows to verify in which areas the researchers have directed their efforts and those that are still underexplored.

Keywords are concise representations of a given text that allow readers to identify its content in advance [17]. The keywords bibliometric data can be used to construct frequency charts of the most used keywords, as well as to elaborate "word clouds".

It is important that the researcher pay attention to keywords similar to terms or expressions already used in the search filtering process. Since these keywords represent obvious information regarding the topic addressed, it is recommended to disregard them to not analyze them in the subsequent analysis. This avoids inconsistencies in the analysis and wasting time and effort of the researcher.

In the case of publications that do not use keywords (something very common in administration journals, for example), the researcher must review the titles (and even the abstracts, in the case of inaccurate titles) to identify terms or expressions that define the main topics covered therein [11, 18].

The word cloud is a practical tool for dimensional visualization of the most used keywords that represent the articles. The Wordle website (www.wordle.net), for instance, provides this tool. When elaborating the word cloud, the researcher should note that expressions such as "Lean Six Sigma" can be understood as three distinct words. To correct this interpretation in the website suggested, the researcher must use the "~" symbol so that the expression will be understood appropriately.

The titles of the articles are bibliometric data used to expose the most cited articles by means of the number of citations received. A simple classification of the articles according to the number of citations can reveal which are the most relevant in the researched literature. Besides the classification of the most cited articles, it is also useful to generate a chart with the evolution of the citations received by the articles over the years. This chart can clarify which articles have increased its importance in the scientific world.

To identify the authors, institutions, journals, and countries most cited in the literature, it is recommended to apply the following steps: (1) visit the Scopus and WoS platforms (logged into your respective accounts) and check in the researcher's list of the authors, institutions, journals, and countries with a minimum number of publications; (2) select the authors, institutions, journals, and countries that meet the requirement set out in step 1; (3) count in the spreadsheet the number of citations received by authors, institutions, journals, and countries; and (4) classify the authors, institutions, journals, and countries according to the highest number of citations received.

It is important to clarify the reason for filtering a minimum number of publications from authors, institutions, journals, and countries applied in step (1). If this filter is not applied, authors who had one or two publications that had a high number of citations will be included in the ranking of the most relevant authors in the literature. This often occurs with researchers who are not specialists in the field of study. For example, one author co-authored two articles that had a high impact on the literature, but the analysis of his research profile reveals that he does not act in the field of study investigated. Therefore, the author of this example may have contributed punctually to the research, but is not a specialist in the subject study.

Tables containing the top 10 authors, institutions, journals, and countries should be generated. In addition to the number of citations received, these may contain other performance information, as presented in **Table 3**.

After obtaining the bibliometric parameters, it is recommended that the bibliometric networks of the research be generated. In this chapter, it is recommended to use VOSviewer software, which will allow the construction of bibliometric networks referring to articles, authors, journals, institutions, and countries based on

Table	Table columns
Most cited articles	Position in the citation ranking, title of the article, authors, journal, year of publication, number of citations, evolution of citations over the years
Most cited authors	Position in the citation ranking, name of the author, institution, H-index, number of publications, number of citations, evolution of citations in the field of study over the years
Most cited institutions	Position in the citation ranking, institution name, country, number of publications, number of citations
Most cited journals	Position in the citation ranking, name of the journal, publishing area, SJR or JCR, ISSN, number of publications, number of citations
Most cited countries	Position in the citation ranking, country name, number of publications, number of citations

Source: Prepared by the authors.

Table 3.
Proposal of additional data for citation ranking tables.

citation, co-citation, co-authorship, and bibliographic coupling. The software also allows quantifying terms, a useful tool to characterize the occurrence of keywords [19]. Examples of networks will be presented and explained in more detail in the next section.

3. Mapping of the state of the art and identification and analysis of gaps and trends of research

The main objective of the analysis of gaps in the literature is to provide the researcher ways to identify opportunities for exploring new relevant topics of a given field of research, as well as studies that have not been fully explored and which require the development of further studies in order to advance the state of the art of a particular theme. Therefore, in this section some types of analysis that may converge in the identification of scientific gaps and research trends will be presented.

3.1 Analysis of authors, countries, institutions, articles, and keywords

The analysis of most cited authors is helpful to the researcher to know the authors who are reference in the area under study and then always be attentive to new studies published by these authors. In this analysis, it is recommended that authors with a minimum number of publications be selected, as this will avoid the selection of authors who are not experts in the field. This type of analysis may indicate to the researcher opportunities for co-orientation partnerships, participation in international research groups, etc.

The analysis of the most cited authors in a theme and their most recent articles on this topic is a way of guiding the development of a bibliometric article that aims at the identification and analysis of gaps and trends. The selection of authors with a minimum number of publications can be done manually in the main research platforms or it can be done by means of the software VOSviewer, which performs the analysis of most cited authors with the option to select the filter of minimum number of publications of a given author.

The analyses of most cited countries and institutions are other possibilities of bibliometric analyses that can help the researcher to direct his academic plans, since the researcher who intends to carry out a research internship must know in advance the countries, institutions, and research centers of excellence in your area. Therefore, the analyses of countries, institutions, and research centers most cited can help researchers to justify possible proposals for research abroad and may also open doors for the establishment of cooperation agreements between students, professors, research groups, and also between universities.

In order to perform these types of analyses, the use of the VOSviewer software is also recommended, since it automatically counts the number of occurrences and citations of each country or institution in a portfolio of documents. In addition, the software is capable of creating several types of networks, such as co-citation and co-authorship, citation of articles, institutions and countries, co-occurrence of keywords, etc. **Figures 5–7** show three forms of visualization of an example of a co-citation network of authors elaborated with the aid of the software VOSviewer, using the data exported by the Scopus platform in ".csv "format type.

Notice in **Figure 5** that the "network visualization" is the simplest display mode, which shows the iterations of co-authorship and formation of some clusters. The second display mode "Overlay visualization" (**Figure 6**) returns a network that brings iterations of co-authorship and formation of clusters and, in addition, brings information of chronological type (see the legend in the bottom right corner of **Figure 6**). Finally, the third display mode (**Figure 7**), although does not show iterations and clusters as the other modes, clearly allows to verify the different densities of the information shown in the network. In this way, it is emphasized that the three display modes are interesting; however, it is important that the researcher knows how to identify the one that can best help the execution of the analyses taking into account the objectives to be reached.

The analysis of the most cited and relevant articles is an important step to help the researcher to develop a theoretical framework of quality for your research project. The researcher needs to be aware of which articles are prominent in the area under study so that documents with important contributions are not left out of the reading portfolio. Likewise, the analysis of the recent articles published by the most cited authors on a given topic can make the identification and analysis of gaps and trends more robust, since it can indicate if the identified gaps have been filled and if there are opportunities for developing new studies.

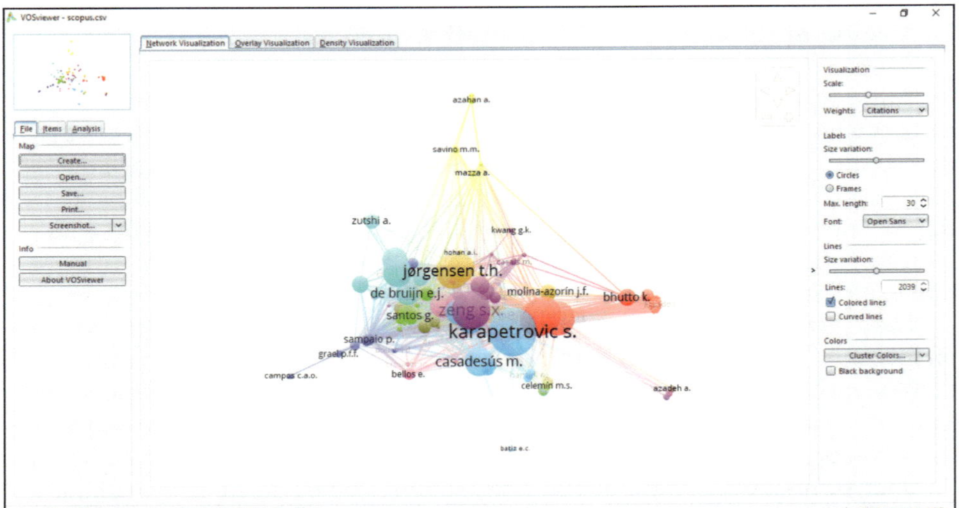

Figure 5.
Author co-citation network in the "network visualization" display mode [15,19].

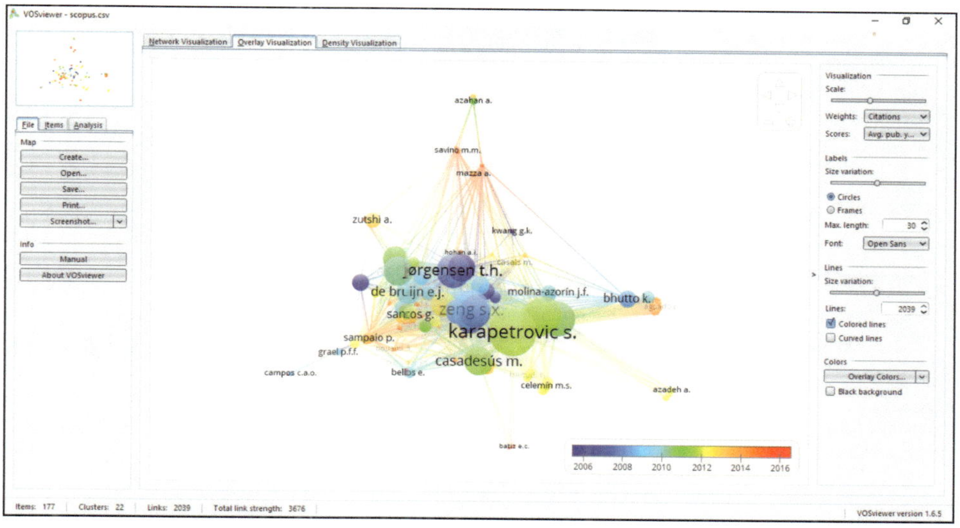

Figure 6.
Author co-citation network in the "overlay visualization" display mode [15,19].

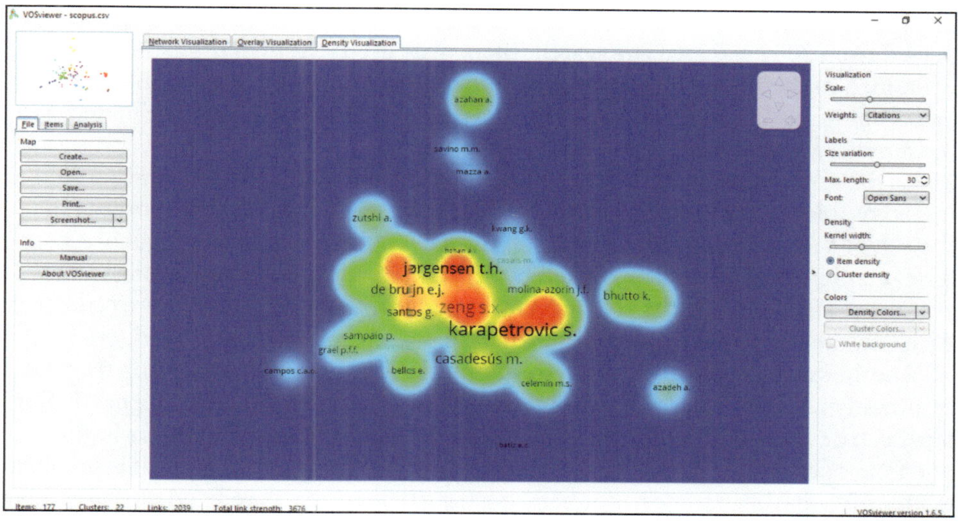

Figure 7.
Author co-citation network in the "density visualization" display mode [15,19].

Researchers are also advised to filter, select, and analyze articles that are most relevant to the topic studied. The option to search for articles by relevance is available on the main research platforms. The results returned in this type of search are in general articles with few citations, since they are commonly newly published. However, to select these articles, the research platforms carry out a projection that identifies the relevant articles based on an evaluation that takes into account the journal in which it was published, research area, average number of citations of similar previous works, etc. Thus, it is important to include the relevant articles in the bibliometric analysis, because they have great potential of impacting on the academic community.

Figure 8 illustrates a possible ranking of the most cited articles for the "business strategy" topic, while **Table 4** presents the objectives, methods, results, and proposal of future studies presented in a selected article for later identification and

#	Most cited articles	Author(s)/(Year)	Author(s) Countries	Total of Citations	Avg. Citations per year	Journal/(ISSN)	SJR (2016)	JCR (2016)	SNIP (2016)	Avg.s 2007	2008	2009	2010	2011	2012	2013	2014	2015	2016
1	Business models, business strategy and innovation	Teece, (2010)	United States	815	101,87	Long Range Planning (0024-6301)	2,697	3,547	2,444	0	0	1	12	44	75	163	212	164	144
2	An institution-based view of internation business strategy: A focus on emerging economies	Peng; Wang; Jiang, (2008)	United States and Hong kong	653	65,30	Journal of International Business Studies (0047-2506)	4,848	5,869	2,958	3	7	25	52	61	92	85	105	118	105
3	The fit between product market strategy and business model: Implications for firm performance	Zott and Amit, (2008)	Spain and India	303	33,67	Strategic Management Journal (0143-2095)	7,651	4,461	3,246	0	2	8	30	28	37	54	63	46	34
4	From strategy to business models and onto tactics	Casadesus and Ricart, (2010)	United States and Spain	291	36,37	Long Range Planning (0024-6301)	2,697	3,547	2,444	0	0	2	8	18	24	55	77	65	42
5	The performance implications of fit among business strategy, marketing organization structure, and strategic behavior	Olson; Slater; Hult, (2005)	United States	271	22,58	Journal of Marketing (0022-2429)	5,947	3,521	5,318	6	22	19	24	34	31	34	40	34	21

Figure 8.
Example of classification of the most cited articles according to the total number of citations. Source: Prepared by the authors.

analysis of gaps and trends. **Table 4** can also help to develop a general perception of a possible timeline and its groups and interactions, which are analyses that will be discussed in the next section.

The classification of the most cited articles in **Figure 8** is in decreasing order, and the ranking was based on the total number of citations accumulated in the period from 2002 to 2016. The search filters were used to return the articles that contained in their titles the word "business strategy" in the "business, management, and accounting,", "social science," "engineering," "environmental science," and "economics, econometrics, and financial" areas.

As the articles of the example in **Figure 8** can be classified in different ways, it is advisable for the researchers to choose to categorize the articles according to their own needs. It should be noted that the list would have another sequence, for example, if the articles presented in **Figure 8** were classified according to the average of citations that the article receives per year or, even, if they were classified based on the impact factors of the journals to which they were published, etc.

Another way to identify gaps in the literature is by means of analyzing the most commonly used keywords in articles on a given topic. The relevance of a particular topic can be measured by the frequency with which the keywords appear in the portfolio of documents analyzed in the bibliometric study. In this way, it is possible to identify whether a topic has already been sufficiently explored and whether there is still the possibility of its further exploration. For example, if a topic is in evidence due to the frequency of a keyword, it may be easier to characterize the existence of gap in the literature, depending on the researcher's experience.

On the other hand, the researcher should be attentive if a keyword that was often used in the articles is today no longer observed with such frequency and regularity, because it can be a sign of a possible exhaustion of a theme in the literature. In order to perform these types of analysis, the use of the software VOSviewer is also recommended, since it automatically counts the number of occurrences of the keywords in the selected articles.

Concerning the identification of gaps by reading the articles, it should be noted that there are two ways to accomplish it. The first one is by analyzing the gaps that are explicit in the text, that is, those that are usually at the conclusion of the articles and, therefore, are easier to identify. Besides, sometimes it is possible that difficulties faced with the conduction of a study can be also considered an explicit gap that may originate new researches.

Among the explicit gaps may also be, for example, those arising from geographical limitations, which are consequences of the natural limitations of the studies.

Author(s)	Objective	Findings	Research method	Literature gaps
Teece [20]	The purpose of this article is to explore the mechanisms by which managers can gauge the required level of organizational agility, deliver it cost-effectively, and relate it to strategy	"Organizational agility" is often treated as an immutable quality, implying that firms need to be in a constant state of transformation. However, this ignores that such transformations, while often essential, come at a cost. They are not always necessary and may not even be possible. This article explores agility at a more fundamental level and relates it more specifically to dynamic capabilities. It demonstrates that it is first essential to understand deep uncertainty, which is ubiquitous in the innovation economy. Business models, dynamic capabilities, and strategy are interdependent. The strength of a firm's dynamic capabilities helps shape its proficiency at business model design. Through its effect on organization design, a business model influences the firm's dynamic capabilities and places bounds on the feasibility of particular strategies	Theoretical; in-depth review of your own literature, based on the new practices and needs of modern markets	While these relationships are understood at a theoretical level, there is a need for future empirical work to flesh out the details. In particular, studies that provide a better understanding of business model innovation, implementation, and change will also shed light on important aspects of dynamic capabilities. Uncertainty is very different from risk, which can be managed using traditional tools and approaches. Strong dynamic capabilities are necessary for fostering the organizational agility necessary to address deep uncertainty, such as that generated by innovation and the associated dynamic competition

Source: Prepared by the authors.

Table 4.
Example of main information to be analyzed in an article and/or review.

In this sense, it is common for researchers to point out in the conclusion of their articles that the expansion of the area of application of the study proves to be a research opportunity. In order to emphasize the relevance of this type of gap, it is recommended to check whether other researches with similar objectives are equally geographically limited. If the geographical limitation is confirmed, a research can be justified by the need to apply the study in other regions, countries, or continents.

The second way to identify gaps in the literature by reading is identifying the implicit gaps in the text. These gaps are harder to identify because they are not highlighted in an explicit manner in the text. Thus, in order to identify implicit gaps, it is important to consider the reader's experience and familiarity with the topic, since researchers with more experiences in a given topic are more likely to identify gaps related to it than less experienced researchers.

3.2 Grouping, timeline, and analysis of interactions

Grouping the topics approached in the bibliometric study in research subareas, conducting the timeline analysis, and searching for similarities between the various groups are important steps to be followed in order to identify gaps and trends of research. The procedures to accomplish this step of the method are presented in this section.

After performing the analysis of gaps in the selected articles and reviews, it is possible to group the main issues addressed in the studied universe. The purpose of this analysis is to identify the structure of the state of the art of the theme, highlighting how its research subareas have evolved over time, how they are developing, and where they are going.

Grouping the various topics into research subareas is a task that requires some degree of mastery on the state of the art of the field studied. For this reason, it is important to develop the analyses of most cited authors and articles, countries and research centers in evidence, etc., because through them it will be possible to extract a rich set of information that will help the perception of similarities, the formation of groups, and the identification of trends of research.

The recommended technique for performing groupings is content analysis, which seeks to identify in a document the frequency with which categories of a given subject are addressed [21]. To determine the categories (or groups), the researcher must identify the most recurring topics (or elements) and account for the frequency that they are addressed directly or indirectly in the articles and reviews analyzed.

To facilitate the visualization of this analysis, a radar chart can be developed. It will show the frequency of occurrence of the elements in the literature and will show the ones that are most recurrent and that, therefore, should lead the formation of the groups. **Figure 9** illustrates the grouping process proposed in this chapter.

It is recommended that the elements with about 70% of occurrence in the portfolio of articles and reviews lead the formation of the groups, since these represent subjects that have been widely discussed in the literature. Once the key elements are

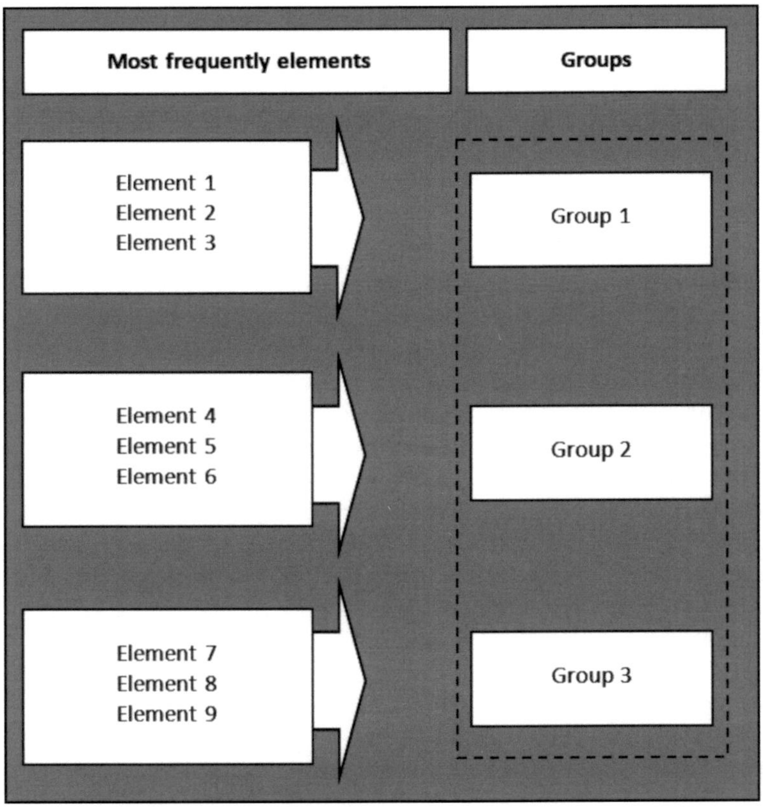

Figure 9.
Grouping process. Source: prepared by the authors.

identified, the other elements should be grouped together based on an analysis of similarities.

It is important to emphasize that the grouping may be led by elements mentioned directly or indirectly in the studies analyzed. Therefore, the group formed from the grouping of elements directly addressed in the texts will be a more mature group, that is, several papers involving the subject have already been published, which shows that the group has already reached a significant degree of development in the state of the art analyzed. On the other hand, the group resulting from the grouping of elements indirectly addressed in the texts may indicate the need to better develop a line of research that, although frequently addressed in the literature, does not yet have specific papers published in this regard.

Once the groups have been created, one must try to understand the evolutionary process of each of them over the years, what are their contributions to the state of the art, and where is the research going in each subarea, evidencing the gaps and trends of each group. The timeline is a tool of analysis that can illustrate from a temporal point of view the general evolution of each group over the years. It also allows the evaluation of the maturity of the research subareas. **Figure 10** shows an example of timeline for the "Integrated Management Systems" search field.

As can be observed in **Figure 10**, the timeline allows researchers to better visualize the contributions of each group for the building of the state of the art, allowing even the comparison of the evolution between the different groups by tracing transverse lines to the horizontal axes of the timeline.

The maturity of each group can be observed according to the volume and distribution of the publications fixed in the axes. In this way, axes with a higher density of work represent the more developed groups, while the more vague axes represent the groups that need more research to be developed.

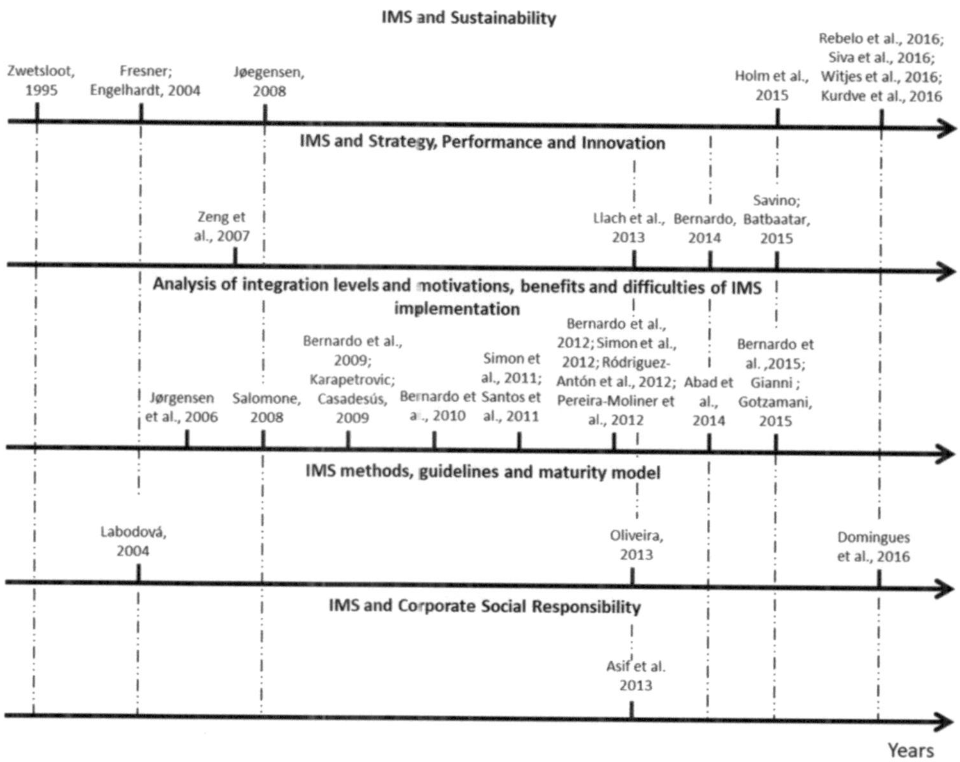

Figure 10.
Timeline to the "Integrated Management Systems" study field [13].

Group	Contribution	Author(s) (year)
IMS and sustainability	The IMS is a driver that can conduct companies to achieve the sustained success	Author1 et al. (2016), Author2 et al. (2016), Author3 et al. (2016), Author4 et al. (2016), Author5 et al. (2015), Author6 (2008), Author7 and Author8 (2004), Author9 (1995)
IMS and strategy, performance and innovation	The IMS is a strategic asset that has positive impact on innovation, financial, operational and marketing firm performance	Author10 and Author11 (2015), Author12 (2014), Author13 et al. (2013), Author14 et al. (2007)
Analysis of integration levels and motivations, benefits and difficulties of IMS implementation	There are different levels of integration (normally three) which characterize the nature of motivations, benefits and difficulties of implementation	Author12 et al. (2015), Author15 and Author16 (2015), Author17 et al. (2014), Author12 et al. (2012), Author18 et al. (2012), Author19 et al. (2012), Author20 et al. (2012), Author18 et al. (2011), Author21 et al. (2011), Author12 et al. (2010), Author12 et al. (2009), Author22 and Author23 (2009), Author24 (2008), Author6 et al. (2006)
IMS methods, guidelines and maturity model	Methods, guidelines and a maturity model are proposed in order to facilitate and/or "normalize" the integration process	Author25 et al. (2016), Author26 (2013), Author27 (2004)
IMS and corporate social responsibility	The IMS structure provides the integration of CSR	Author28 et al. (2013)

Table 5.
Group analysis [13].

In addition to the time line, the groups and their respective contributions can be presented as shown in **Table 5**.

It can be seen in **Table 5** that the 30 articles analyzed were classified into 5 groups, each one adding value to an important area of the state of the art on "Integrated Management Systems."

After grouping the topics and understanding the particularities of each group, it is recommended to identify if there is any relation between them, that is, if there is a structure of evolution according to which one group gave support to the development of another. **Figure 11** shows a map of interactions with the interactions between the research groups on "Integrated Management Systems."

As shown in **Figure 11**, it is common for the more mature groups to influence the development of more recent ones, as the publications of a group can add important contributions and indicate gaps that may create trends of research to advance the state of the art of a given study field as a whole. It is important that the synergies between the groups and the pathway of formation and development of the state of the art are indicated in the map of interactions.

The analysis of interactions is a final analysis that must be conducted with a systemic view, because from it the researcher can perceive interaction relationships with potential to give rise to groups with original research proposals. Upon reaching this point of application of the method, the researcher is expected to know the particularities of the field under study and the main groups belonging to it, so that the analyses performed previously will provide support for the identification of relations of interactions between the various groups.

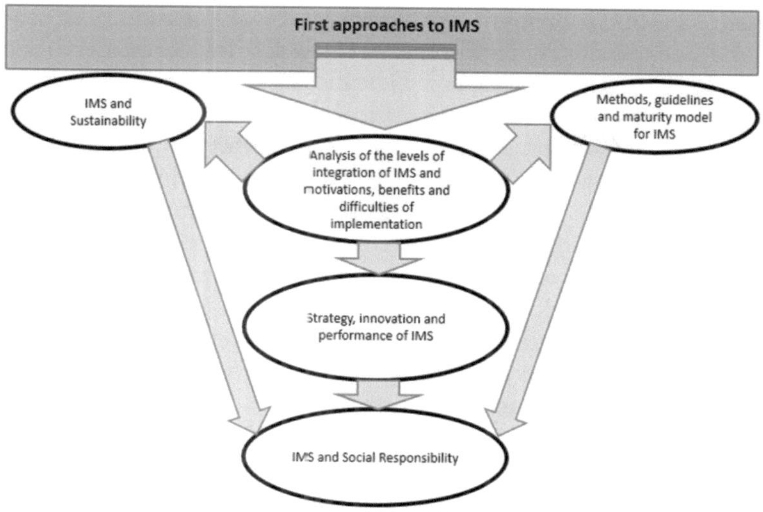

Figure 11.
Map of interactions. Adapted from [13].

4. Conclusions

In this chapter, a method of bibliometric analysis was proposed in order to help researchers develop a relevant research project based on the mapping of the state of the art of a given topic and the identification, grouping, and analysis of gaps and trends of research.

It was observed that the choice of the scientific research platform to be used in the study is one of the actions that has a significant impact in the bibliometric analysis and, therefore, must be careful and well planned so that the research will return assertive results and reworking will not be necessary in the subsequent stages of the analysis. In addition, it was verified that it is necessary to establish criteria to perform the search of the articles, which must take into account the research topic, the objectives of the study, and the limits of the research field.

In the proposed method, the mapping of the state of the art should be initiated with the definition of the bibliometric parameters by the researcher, which has to be consistent with those available in the scientific research platforms. By analyzing the data mined, it is possible to compare the performance of the literature according to each platform to corroborate, complement, or refute results.

It is concluded that the use of data extracted from two or more platforms can result in a more robust and consistent bibliometric analysis. However, it is possible that the researcher faces difficulties in the integration stage of the data. In this sense, it is important to highlight that although there are computational tools that help the integration of this data, these still need great improvements, demanding extreme attention of the researcher in the process of mining and analysis of the data.

The analyses presented in this chapter are important elements to expose and explain the scientific gaps present in the literature that can base research projects. Therefore, it can be concluded that the method presented is essential to help researchers to develop their research in a way that they actually bring out significant contributions to the literature. It is also concluded that the application of this method can result in the expansion of the frontiers of science by promoting the investigation of relevant and avant-garde topics.

The main scientific contribution of this chapter is the possibility of using the proposed method to help the development of new studies, based on bibliometric analyses aimed at the identification of scientific gaps and trends, thus encouraging the development and expansion of the state of the art of various fields of research.

It is also worth noting that the mapping of the state of the art and the identification of scientific gaps and trends can lead the researcher to develop studies whose results are important advances in the development of a technology, technique, or scientific area. In this way, it is notorious that the presented method can aid in the process of transformation of a scientific project into a workable product, being this the main applied contribution of this study.

Finally, it should be pointed out that the results achieved with the application of the proposed method may vary according to the experience and familiarity of the researcher with the scientific area under study.

Acknowledgements

This work was supported by the Brazilian Council for Scientific and Technological Development (CNPq), Coordination for the Improvement of Higher Education Personnel (CAPES), and São Paulo Research Foundation (FAPESP) under the Grant numbers 2016/20160-0 and 2017/18304-7.

Author details

Otávio José de Oliveira[1]*, Fabio Francisco da Silva[2], Fernando Juliani[1], Luis César Ferreira Motta Barbosa[1] and Thaís Vieira Nunhes[1]

1 São Paulo State University, Guaratinguetá, Brazil

2 Federal Institute of Education, Science and Technology of Goiás, Valparaíso de Goiás, Brazil

*Address all correspondence to: otaviodeoliveira@uol.com.br

References

[1] Dragos CM, Dragos SL. Bibliometric approach of factors affecting scientific productivity in environmental sciences and ecology. Science of the Total Environment. 2013;**449**:184-188. DOI: 10.1016/j.scitotenv.2013.01.057

[2] Bornmann L, Leydesdorff L. Scientometrics in a changing research landscape. Science & Society. 2014;**15**:1228-1231. DOI: https://10.15252/embr.201439608

[3] Gumpenberger C, Wieland M, Gorraiz J. Bibliometric practices and activities at the University of Vienna. Library Management. 2012;**33**:74-183. DOI: 10.1108/01435121211217199

[4] Campbell D, Picard-Aitken M, Côté G, Caruso J, Valentim R, Edmonds S, et al. Bibliometrics as a performance measurement tool for research evaluation: The case of research funded by the national cancer institute of Canada. American Journal of Evaluation. 2010;**31**:66-83. DOI: 10.1177/1098214009354774

[5] Vogel R. What happened to the public organization? A Bibliometric Analysis of public administration and organization studies. American Review of Public Administration. 2014;**44**:383-408. DOI: 10.1177/0275074012470867

[6] Gläser J, Laudel G. A bibliometric reconstruction of research trails for qualitative investigations of scientific innovations. Historical Social Research. 2015;**40**:299-330. DOI: 10.12759/hsr.40.2015.3.299-330

[7] Bornmann L. How are excellent (highly cited) papers defined in bibliometrics? A quantitative analysis of the literature. Research Evaluation. 2014;**23**:166-173. DOI: 10.1093/reseval/rvu002

[8] Brueton VC, Vale CL, Choodari-Oskooei B, Jinks R, Tierney JF. Measuring the impact of methodological research: A framework and methods to identify evidence of impact. Trials. 2014;**15**:1-7. DOI: 10.1186/1745-6215-15-464

[9] Abrizah A, Zainab AN, Kiran K, Raj RG. LIS journals scientific impact and subject categorization: A comparison between Web of Science and Scopus. Scientometrics. 2013;**94**:721-740

[10] Bartol T, Budimir G, Dekleva-Smrekar D, Pusnik M, Juznic P. Assessment of research fields in Scopus and Web of Science in the view ofnational research evaluation in Slovenia. Scientometrics. 2014;**98**:1491-1504. DOI: 10.1007/s11192-013-1148-8

[11] Juliani F, Oliveira OJ. State of research on public service management: Identifying scientific gaps from a bibliometric study. International Journal of Information Management. 2016;**36**:1033-1041. DOI: 10.1016/j.ijinfomgt.2016.07.003

[12] Filser L, Silva FF, Oliveira OJ. State of research and future research tendencies in lean healthcare: A bibliometric analysis. Scientometrics. 2017;**112**:799-816

[13] Nunhes TV, Motta LCF, Oliveira OJ. Evolution of integrated management systems research on the Journal of Cleaner Production: Identification of contributions and gaps in the literature. Journal of Cleaner Production. 2016;**139**:1234-1244

[14] Garza-reys JA. Lean and green—A systematic review of the state of the art literature. Journal of Cleaner Production. 2015;**102**:18-29

[15] Scopus [Internet]. 2018. Available from: https://www.scopus.com [Accessed: 2018-01-02]

[16] WoS [Internet]. 2018. Available from: https://webofknowledge.com [Accessed: 2018-01-02]

[17] Ercan G, Cicekli I. Using lexical chains for keyword extraction. Information Processing and Management. 2007;**43**:1705-1714

[18] Gil-Leiva I, Alonso-Arroyo A. Keywords given by authors of scientific articles in database descriptors. Journal of the American Society for Information Science and Technology. 2007;**58**:1175-1187

[19] VOSViewer [Internet]. 2018. Available from: http://www.vosviewer.com [Accessed: 2018-01-05]

[20] Teece DJ. Business models and dynamic capabilities. Long Range Planning. 2018;**51**:40-49

[21] Scott J, Analysis C. In: Jupp V, editor. The Sage Dictionary of Social Research Methods. 1st ed. London: Sage; 2006. pp. 79-249

Chapter 4

Detection and Characterization of E-Health Research: A Bibliometrics (2001–2016)

Zhiyong Liu, Jianjun Su and Lei Ji

Abstract

E-health is the use of ICT to improve the ability to treat patients, facilitate behavior change, and improve health. It has many benefits like healthcare cost reduction, convenience for users, and health system improvement. Several literature reviews have included one part or the other of the field, but an overall review is lacking possibly due to the field's constant evolution. An overview of E-health research is needed. We selected the related literature on E-health downloaded from Web of Science and PubMed as data source and used the visualization analysis function of CiteSpace. Literature information would be converted into precise mapping knowledge domain. Through further analysis of mappings, we explored the theoretical framework and the forefront in the field of E-health. Our study shows that over the past 15 years, the USA, England, and Australia were the top three countries that published the largest number of papers. Researches about Internet technology, telemedicine (m-health), and healthcare lay the basis of E-health research development. Particularly, m-health, health system management, and experimental intervention have emerged and formed the new study frontier in the recent 3–5 years. With the advancement of E-health projects, an increasing number of scholars have been studying the commercialization of E-health.

Keywords: E-health, bibliometrics, visualization analysis, CiteSpace

1. Background

Advances in information and communication technology (ICT) and the dissemination of network data processing created a new environment of universal access to information and globalization of communications, businesses, and services. In the health sector, a variety of new ICTs are implemented to improve the efficiency of all levels of healthcare. E-health—or digital health—is the use of ICT to improve the ability to treat patients, facilitate behavior change, and improve health. Many benefits of E-health have been presented, including cost reduction and convenience for users [1, 2], reduction of health service costs and improving health service quality [3, 4], reaching isolated or stigmatized groups, timeliness of access to the Internet [5], increasing user and supplier control of the E-health intervention [6], and changing government policy making [1]. E-health is making healthcare more efficient while allowing patients and professionals to access and manage data in ways that were previously impossible [7]. Thus, E-health does not specifically refer to a certain subject. It is an application area where many subjects are associated such as clinical informatics, health informatics, electronic health record, consumer health informatics, and various Internet-based technologies and services [8].

According to Faber, Mitchell coined the term E-health in 1999 [9]. The study of E-health has attracted research interest after it was used by the World Health Organization (WHO) [10]. First, some researchers raise the theory that E-health communication may have immense potential to promote behavior changes through unique features such as mass customization, interactivity, and convenience. As a result, it can help improve the quality of medical care and lower the cost [11, 12]. On the basis of these theories, many researches have been conducted to confirm the advantages and benefits of E-health, such as “automatic-sleep classification program” research and “E-health intervention model designing” [13, 14], challenges in establishing a national databank of anonymized person-based records, and randomized controlled trial of web-guided approach [15–17]. Published articles in related fields are on the rise year by year (**Figure 1**), and many countries have also raised programs, Europe “e-Health Action Plan 2004–2010” and “e-Health Action Plan 2012–2020” and the USA “Federal Health IT Strategic Plan (2015–2020),” on the development of health information systems. The United Kingdom “Health and Social Care Act 2012” proposed that we need to reform healthcare and take the advantage of information technologies to improve the quality of patient care [18–20]. It informs us that combining health work with ICT is the trend of medicine development since medicine and health are the basis of stable development for a country.

As for E-health researches, there are several main topics: (1) Consensus and standardization of E-health research. (2) Evaluation methods and challenges—proper evaluation methods are needed to establish E-health quality and efficiency evaluation model [21, 22]. (3) Quality, value, and future trends—as most people

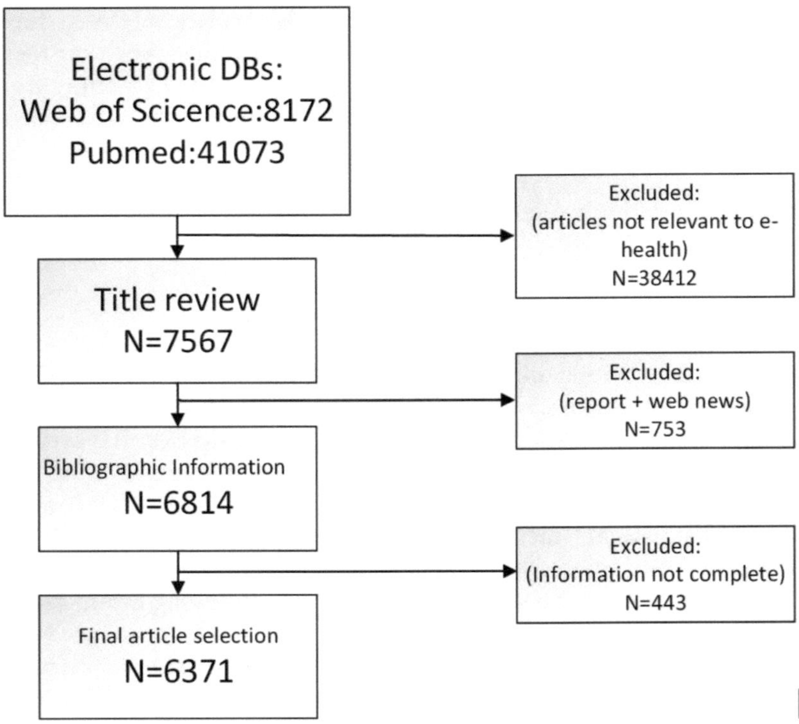

Figure 1.
Flow chart of the literature.

think, E-health application is cost-effective and efficient and will improve qualities of clinical work [23–25]. The academic literature has primarily focused on issues in the adoption and diffusion of specific E-health technologies, and only a few papers concern on the development of E-health subject [26]. This leads to the current state that although some literature reviews cover one part or the other of the field [27, 28], an overall picture is still missing which is possibly due to the field's constant evolution. Besides, coherence of these researches is poor, and the interaction between scholars is not enough, making it difficult to reach a consensus about E-health research.

We explore the law of E-health discipline development using the scientific metrology, social network analysis, and information visualization technology. Progressively synthesized co-citation networks are constructed and visualized to aid visual analytic studies of the domain's structural and dynamic patterns and trends [29]. The formation of E-health, hot topics evolution, and trend of this research field being explored is achieved.

This study aims to present an analytical review on the state of E-health research. A review framework composed of multiple research methods is developed and applied to yield a broad coverage of E-health research. We explore the distribution of E-health hot topics and probe the research frontier by bibliometric methods. The evolution of different topics is evaluated and some research directions are proposed.

2. Methods and tools

2.1 Data source

Web of Science core collection is used as data sources. We summarized the scope of E-health, and developed the following search query according to the results of literature research (**Table 1**). We selected the search term to retrieve all relevant literatures for 15 years, and 6371 documents were retrieved in total.

		Search query	Number of hits
WOS	#1	TS = (Clinical decision support system) OR TS = (Health informatics) OR TS = (Medical research using grids) OR TS = (healthcare information systems)	23,184
	#2	TS = (Clinical Informatics) AND #1	2209
	#3	TS = ((electronic health record) or EHR or cpoe or (computerized physician order entry) or e-prescribing)	18,034
	#4	TS = (CONSUMER HEALTH INFORMATICS)	409
	#5	TS = ((health knowledge management) or (decision aids for patients) or (virtual healthcare teams))	17,993
	#6	TS = (telemedicine or mhealth or m-health or wireless networks or (vr technology) or cloud-computing or (self-monitoring healthcare devices) or (health surveillance systems) or (e-mental health))	206,209
	#7	TS = cyber medicine	26
	#8	TI = (ehealth or (e-health) or (E-Health) or EHealth or EHEALTH or E-HEALTH or (electronic health))	9484
	#9	TI = health and (big data)	283
	#10	TS = health and (big data)	3558

		Search query	Number of hits
	#11	#9 and #10	283
	#12	#7 OR #6 OR #5 OR #4 OR #3 OR #2 OR #1	241,715
	#13	#12 or #11 and #8	8172
PubMed	#1	(((ehealth OR (e-health) OR (e-health) OR ehealth OR ehealth OR e-health OR (electronic health)) title/abstract)) AND (((((((((Clinical decision support system[Title/Abstract]) OR Health informatics[Title/Abstract]) OR Medical research using grids[Title/Abstract]) OR healthcare information systems[Title/Abstract])) OR ((Clinical Informatics[Title/Abstract]) AND ((((Clinical decision support system [Title/Abstract]) OR Health informatics[Title/Abstract]) OR Medical research using grids[Title/Abstract]) OR healthcare information systems [Title/Abstract]))) OR ((clinical informatics) AND ((((Clinical decision support system[Title/Abstract]) OR Health informatics[Title/Abstract]) OR Medical research using grids[Title/Abstract]) OR healthcare information systems[Title/Abstract]))) OR (((electronic health record [Title/Abstract]) OR cpoe[Title/Abstract]) OR e-prescribing[Title/Abstract])) OR CONSUMER HEALTH INFORMATICS[Title/Abstract]) OR ((((health knowledge management[Title/Abstract]) OR decision aids for patients[Title/Abstract]) OR virtual healthcare teams[Title/Abstract])) OR ((telemedicine OR health OR m-health OR wireless networks OR (vr technology) OR cloud-computing OR (self-monitoring healthcare devices) OR (health surveillance systems) OR (e-mental health)) title/abstract))	41,073

Table 1.
Search query for this study.

2.2 Methods and tools

Information visualization is an analytical method which can realize the interactive visualization analysis on abstract data and enhance people's perception of the abstract information [30]. To some extent, information visualization offers a quick independent, scientific judgment of the objective evidences [31]. CiteSpace, UCINET, Pajek, His cite, and Ref Viez 3 are software that researchers used mostly to do information visualization analysis, among which CiteSpace is the most popular one [32, 33]. CiteSpace, a Java-based application developed by Chaomei Chen professor who is a Changjiang Scholar from Dalian University of Technology, can display the abstracted data in the visual form and facilitates further data analysis, rule discovery, and decision-making. It is easy to use and its visualization results are excellent. In this paper, we determined the discipline layout and hot spots about E-health in a specific period based on SCI and CiteSpace.

3. Results

3.1 Brief descriptions of E-health development

3.1.1 Number of articles published

As **Figure 2** shows, the histogram denoted quantity of E-health research, and the line chart shows the literature accounted to the total each year. In general, the quantity of the published literature showed an increasing trend with the average

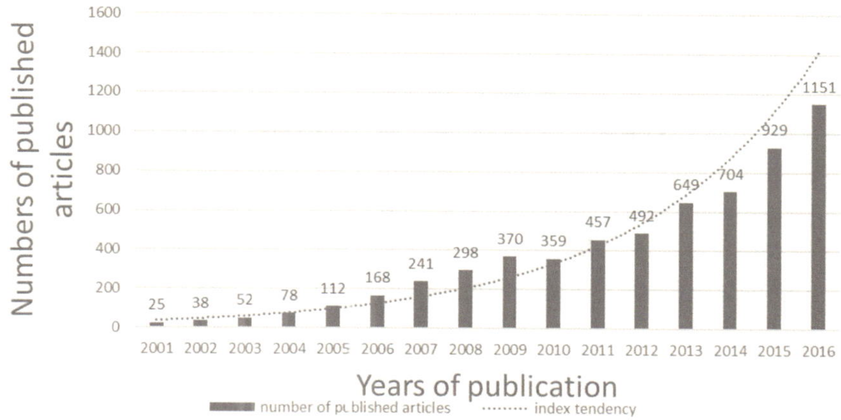

Figure 2.
The number of articles published each year.

annual growth rate of 29.93% from 2001 to 2016. In detail, we saw two inflection points in 2005 and 2010. Considering the quantity and proportion trend of the literature, we divided the whole research time into three parts which are listed as 2001–2005, 2006–2010, and 2011–2016.

Reasons for the above trend have two aspects. First, they are associated with some pivotal view point. Eysenbach, G and WEBB, TL published their important literature in 2005 and 2010. They are both authorities in E-health research [7, 34]. Therefore, the quantity of published literature began to rise in these years. Second, developing technology and government attaching importance to medical research contributed a lot. The development of E-health depended on science and technology progress. Many governments have different preferential policies for health science research and Internet communication techniques which promoted E-health research.

3.1.2 Country analysis

Figure 3 shows the published number of key nodes and the influence degree of relevant researchers concretely. Centrality is an index used to measure the

Figure 3.
Visualization map of countries.

Frequency	Centrality	Country	Rank
1158	0.28	USA	1
486	0.17	England	2
480	0.15	Australia	3
434	0.16	Canada	4
430	0.08	Netherlands	5
415	0.11	Germany	6
323	0.1	Spain	7
273	0.04	Italy	8
195	0.02	Austria	9
180	0.12	France	10
161	0.05	Sweden	11
154	0.01	People's of Republic China	12
143	0.08	Switzerland	13

Table 2.
High-frequency countries.

importance of a node in the whole network. It is more likely that the node is the key point in the network if the centrality is big. As shown in **Table 2**, USA's published quantity was the most in the top 13 countries. In detail, America published 1158 papers, which accounted for one-fifth of all literature from 2001 to 2016, whereas China was in the twelfth place. China published 154 papers, accounting for only 2.6%. Above countries had the centrality from 2002 to 2004, among which the USA have had it earlier in 2002 and CHINA in 2004. As for the centrality value, the USA, England, and Australia were the top three, and their researchers had a major influence on the field of E-health at the same time. Besides, the influence of China is quite weak because of its low-value centrality.

3.1.3 Research directions

Every article has multiple research directions, but after statistically ranking, the top 10 directions were: healthcare science and service, computer science, medical informatics, engineering, public environmental occupational health, telecommunications, psychology, general internal medicine, and information science library science. In addition, these articles also involve some elements of clinical areas such as nursing, cancer treatment, pharmacy, and science and technology development (**Table 3**). The top four research directions are healthcare science and services, computer science, medical informatics, and engineering, accounting for more than 100%, which means all the literature is concerned with the four research directions, so it is suggested that these four research directions are the theoretical basis of E-health research.

3.1.4 Authorship analysis

As for the publishing frequency of authors, their publishing situation was the same as the regarding countries'. We try to strengthen the cooperation between authors to serve the E-health and those producing more relevant output. As shown

Research directions	Frequency	Rank
Healthcare science and service	1919	1
Computer science	1904	2
Medical informatics	1439	3
Engineering	1095	4
Telecommunications	411	5
Public environmental occupational health	367	6
Psychology	242	7
General internal medicine	213	8
Information science library science	183	9
Nursing	149	10

Table 3.
Research directions.

in **Figure 4** and **Table 4**, the top five authors did not cooperate with others directly. It indicated that they focused on different topics and all of them were leaders in their research directions. Bernd Blobel was the top and he published 35 papers. He works at University Hospital Regensburg. By studying the privacy and security of some E-health system, he could analyze and design of advanced health systems properly [35–37]. Gunter Schreier concerns that using mobile devices or communication technologies provide huge opportunities for home monitoring applications [38]. He found that different types of data acquisition technologies have an important effect on patients' willingness to participate in telehealth programs in the long term [39]. JJPC Rodrigues works at the University of Beira Interior. He mainly studied the application effect of different kinds of wireless sensor networks in the

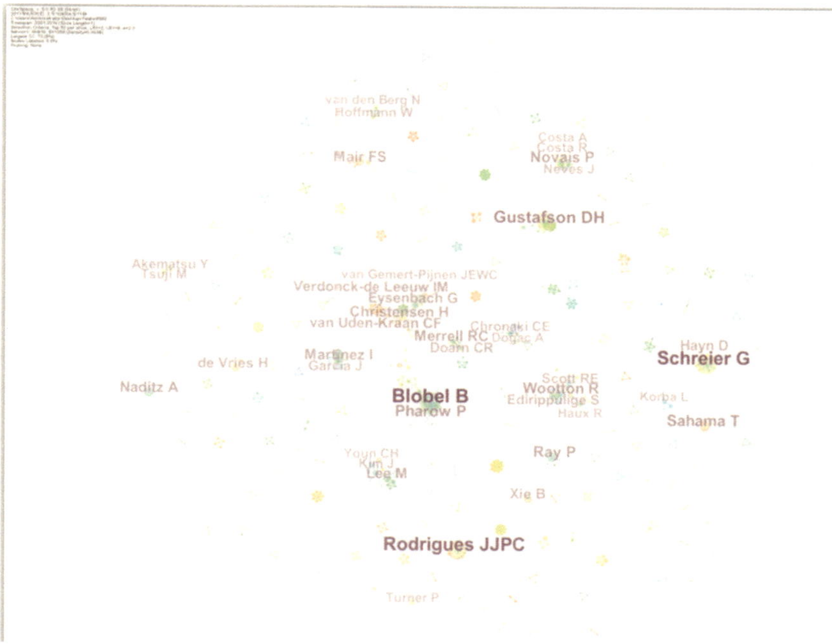

Figure 4.
Visualization map of authors.

Authors	Frequency	Rank
Blobel B	35	1
Schreier G	33	2
Rodrigues JJPC	29	3
Gustafson DH	28	4
Eysenbach G	22	5

Table 4.
High-frequency authors.

medical field. In the last 15 years, he proposed some network solutions, such as IP-based wireless sensor network, biofeedback data visualization for body sensor networks, real-time query processing optimization for wireless sensor network, and so on [40–42]. Gustafson typical papers are concerned with the research around consumer health informatics which influence on how patients or potential patients get health knowledge they need [43]. As for Eysenbach, he is the founder of E-health field, and he proposed the concept of E-health in 2002. In the subsequent time, he researched on the quality of electronic health information, Internet access to health information, and evaluation of E-health-related program [44–46]. According to the number of citations, Eysenbach is one of the most important core authors in E-health research. The focus of these five authors is not the same, but from the visualization map, their research direction all represents hot spots in this period.

3.2 Research focus analysis and frontier analysis in E-health research

3.2.1 Research focus analysis

Research hot spots are issues or special directions studied by lots of people in recent years. Keywords, a highly generalized summary, and important index of papers are the core of academic papers. Therefore, we could get the research hot spots and the main subjects of one study area by analyzing the change trend and characteristic of the keyword frequency (**Figure 5**).

Due to the function of CiteSpace, the bigger the size of node is, the more important the node in the visualization map is. It is obvious that some keywords [Internet, telemedicine (m-health), technology, randomized controlled trial, management, and system] have a quite bigger size than others. Besides, considering that our research topic belongs to medical study, we could speculate that telemedicine, randomized controlled trial, health system, health management, and applying Internet-related technology in medical field have become the research hot spots and the main subjects in the study of most scholars from 2001 to 2016.

Seeing from the frequency of keywords, we can broadly divide the E-health research into several main subjects. “Internet technology” is the first one, which is the combination of “Internet” and “technology.” E-health is the ICT in the field of healthcare, so the Internet technology development is driving force of E-health [17]. “Telemedicine,” the second subject, appeared 618. It refers to the provision of remote clinical services via real-time two-way communication between the patient and the healthcare provider by using electronic audio and visual means. “Telehealth,” “m-health,” and “communication” belong to it, which mainly concern on whether telemedicine or m-health could help improve the efficiency of individual access to medical services to solve the existing problems [47, 48]. “Randomized controlled trial,” the third one, is research method and one kind of intervention. These clusters concentrate on proving the advantages and disadvantages of E-health

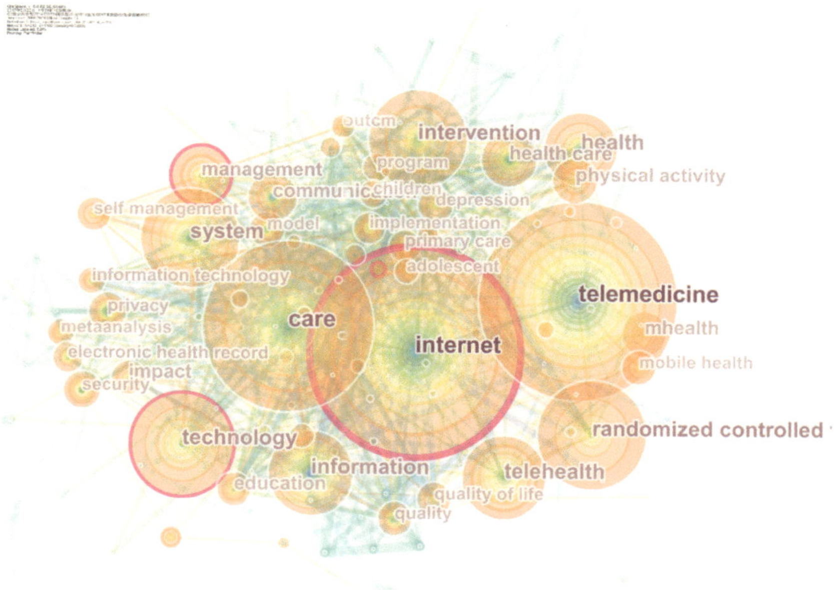

Figure 5.
Visualization of hot topics in 2001–2016.

programs. Fourthly, papers researching "healthcare field" focus on E-health application like electronic health record and attributes such as security, privacy, and interoperability [49]. With the promotion of information network technology development, the main task of the next phase is how to ensure the efficiency of E-health system data storage security, transmission, ease of use, and privacy protection. "Health management," the fifth one, is an abstract conception. Any keywords associated with management can be divided into this class such as self-management, adherence, and mental health management [17, 50, 51].

3.2.2 Visualization of hot topics evolution

To explore the degree of concern of the international E-health research, we divided it into three periods: from 2001 to 2005, 2006 to 2010, and 2011 to 2016. The frequency of keywords has been counted as shown in **Table 5**. Similar to the above method, we get the visualization maps of keywords in different times, as shown in **Figures 6–8**.

In Atlas of visualization, the three stages of topics evolution show a gradual trend of convergence. In 2001–2005, the link intensity among high-frequency keywords was low. The study of E-health was at an exploratory stage, and research direction is scattered as scholars had not yet formed a complete theoretical system. With the emergence of E-health concepts raising academic great interest, scholars considered using network communication technology can greatly improve the quality of medical service and reduce healthcare costs. However, they also doubted whether it determined the actual role, which focused them on the theoretical exploration and the possibility of assessment of E-health [45, 52–54]. In 2006–2010, with the Internet explosively developing and governments attaching more importance to E-health gradually, some medical items based on network technology entered the implementation phase. Scholars tried to evaluate implementation of these projects from visual map aspects. The formation of E-health research prototype has an important connection with the Internet, telemedicine, and care.

2001–2005		2006–2010		2011–2016	
Keywords	**Frequency**	**Keywords**	**Frequency**	**Keywords**	**Frequency**
Telemedicine	39	Telemedicine	163	Internet	440
Internet	37	Internet	151	Care	416
Information	20	Care	92	Telemedicine	416
System	18	Information	73	Randomized controlled trial	323
Care	16	System	71	Intervention	281
Health information	10	Telehealth	59	Technology	278
Quality	10	Quality	51	M-health	251
Education	9	Technology	48	System	247
Information technology	8	Health	47	Telehealth	213
Management	7	Healthcare	47	Health	204

Table 5.
Frequency of keywords in different periods.

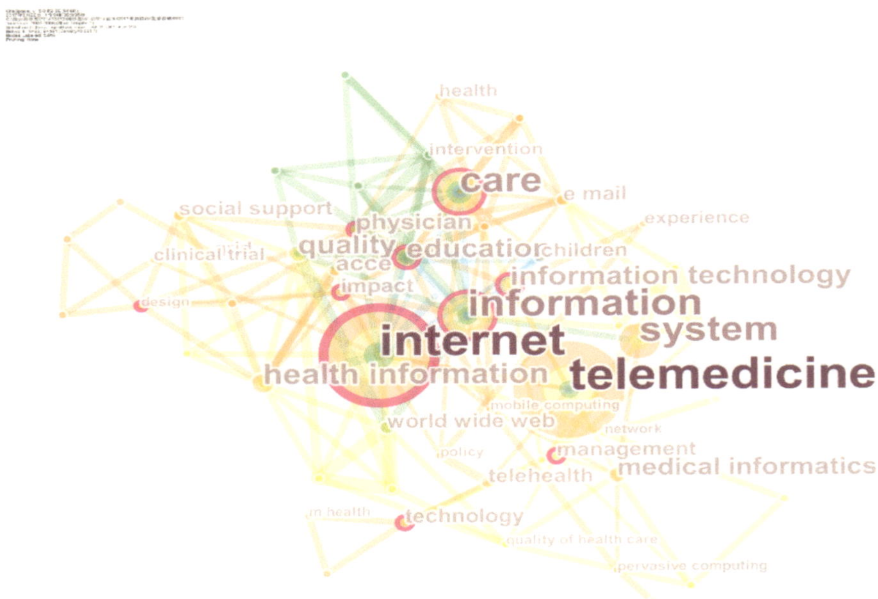

Figure 6.
Visualization of hot topics in 2001–2005.

Scholars thought that the core was the Internet, telemedicine, and care. This provided a point of reference standard for future research directions and reduced misuse and abuse of the concept [44, 55–58]. In 2011–2016, visual maps showed that the core keywords were still the Internet, telemedicine, and care. The map of central tendency is obvious but there had been significant changes. M-health, system management, and randomized controlled trial suddenly broke out, which respectively reflected three characteristics of E-health research: mobile, systematic, and precision. The popularity of mobile and wearable devices greatly accelerated the development process of E-health. Systematic management of the healthcare system can effectively improve the quality of medical services. Precision means

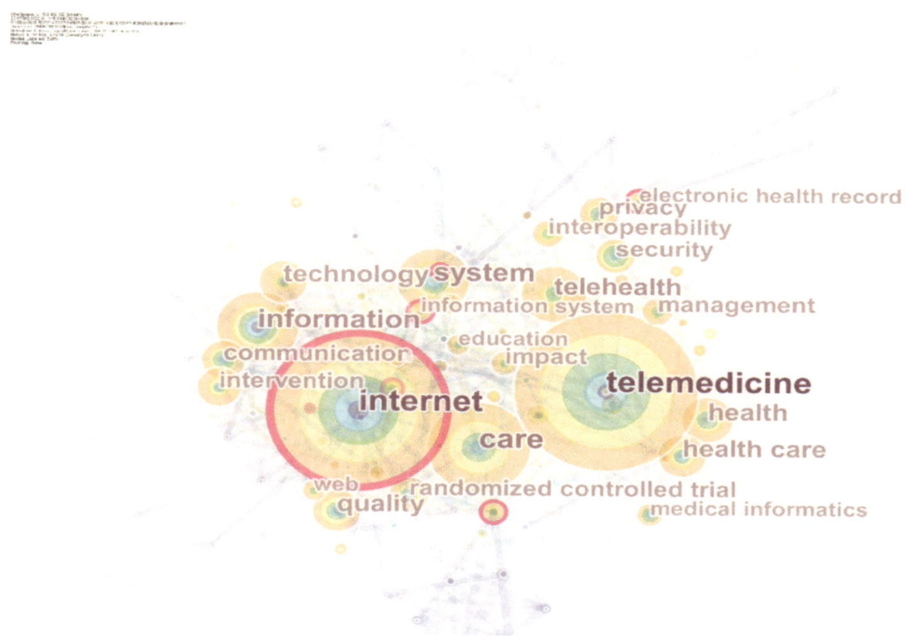

Figure 7.
Visualization of hot topics in 2006–2010.

Figure 8.
Visualization of hot topics in 2011–2016.

researchers used random control experiments and other scientific methods to assess E-health to obtain scientific outputs [59, 60]. In addition, the keyword "big data" began to appear in the knowledge map, indicating that scholars began to study the application of health data technology to promote E-health-related research projects. Application of big data technology can help solve the problem that medical field data volume, various, and grows rapidly to deal with.

The evolution of topics in **Figures 6–8** and **Table 5** can be divided into several classes: continuous topics, emerging topics, and disappearing topics.

Continuous topics: telemedicine, Internet technology, and care are continuous academic focus of research topics. From the point of view of clusters each year, telemedicine, Internet technology, and care focus on different research topics in the last decade. The main direction of telemedicine research is to determine the initial authoritative definition and unify communication standard [61].The aim of mid-term is to assess the effect of the recent literature, and the aim of recent time is to review telemedicine research from the perspective of human society. Internet technology which functioned as support of the development of E-health technology in recent years has undergone tremendous changes. Scholars began to explore the possibility of using a network to pass health information, using network storage to transfer data, and analyzing the advantages and disadvantages of doing so. Then, they gradually changed to focus on the user network information literacy and healthy relationship, which pointed out that information literacy is to enhance users' ability to understand E-health for further development [62]. Electronic health records are the most direct and most important solutions for problems such as how to build a unified specification and how to help different medical workers when they cannot communicate directly. Research focus gradually changed the use of electronic health record information, medical research, and health information so that they maximize the effectiveness of change.

Emerging topics, including health technology, information literacy, and cloud computing, have developed rapidly in a few years. Relatively speaking, mobile health technology and information literacy were at the heart of co-occurrence analysis in recent years. Improvements of the Internet and other information technologies and increasing researchers' knowledge promote the application of E-health. Earlier E-health applications and services are based on computer terminals, but portable monitor cannot do that with the advances in mobile technology in recent years. Thus, the use of mobile devices in health and disease management or monitoring the user's health condition has attracted great concern [63]. In previous studies, researchers found that different users get different abilities to accept the electronic health information, which has significant impact on the development of E-health. Therefore, some scholars have done some research in information literacy [64].

Cloud computing is an emerging technology based on Internet computing in which shared resources are provided on the Internet to other users on demand. Basically, cloud is a synonym for the Internet and composed of clusters of

Frequency	Burst	Author	Year	Title	Journal source
17	9.52	van Gemert-Pijnen JEWC	2011	"A holistic framework to improve the uptake and impact of eHealth technologies"	Journal of Medical Internet Research
15	9.40	Donkin L	2011	"A systematic review of the impact of adherence on the effectiveness of e-therapies"	Journal of Medical Internet Research
20	8.42	Mair FS	2012	"Factors that promote or inhibit the implementation of E-health system: an explanatory systematic review"	Patient Education and Counseling

Table 6.
Document bursting information.

computers working upon distributed systems that provide service in real time over a network. Cloud computing is massively scalable which provides a superior user experience and is characterized by new Internet-driven economics [65]. Once established a unified exchange standard is used to do real-time exchange; the amount of data analyzer will face is enormous, so using cloud computing technologies to process these data would be a satisfactory solution.

Nonetheless, studies regarding information security, privacy, and IT policies had decreased gradually in these three periods.

3.3 Research frontier analysis

The concept of research frontier was introduced by Price. It is used to describe a trend in the field of research. Price uses his own definition of indicators and watches the trends of the article citations according to these indicators [66]. Research frontier is a dynamic concept. The cited articles containing the contents of research front are the knowledge base, and research front is based on these articles. Emergence refers to the rate of change of cited frequency, which can be considered that the content of some emergent literature is discussed form research frontiers. To detect research frontier, we need to analyze the content of citing articles, burst words, and burst literature. CiteSpace provide us a method—Citing articles Cluster, which is the base of identifying clustering-edge [67]. By doing content analysis and clustering, according to Visual analysis results CiteSpace outputted, we can determine the forefront of research in the field of E-health research.

We do co-citation network process, get burst information of literature, and use the burstness at the right of the software to view the strength of emergent literature and emergent time distribution (**Figure 9**).

The first column in **Figure 6** indicates cited emergent literature and strength, representing emergent index. The higher the index is, the more focused cited literature is. The right place in the figure indicates the time literature emergence.

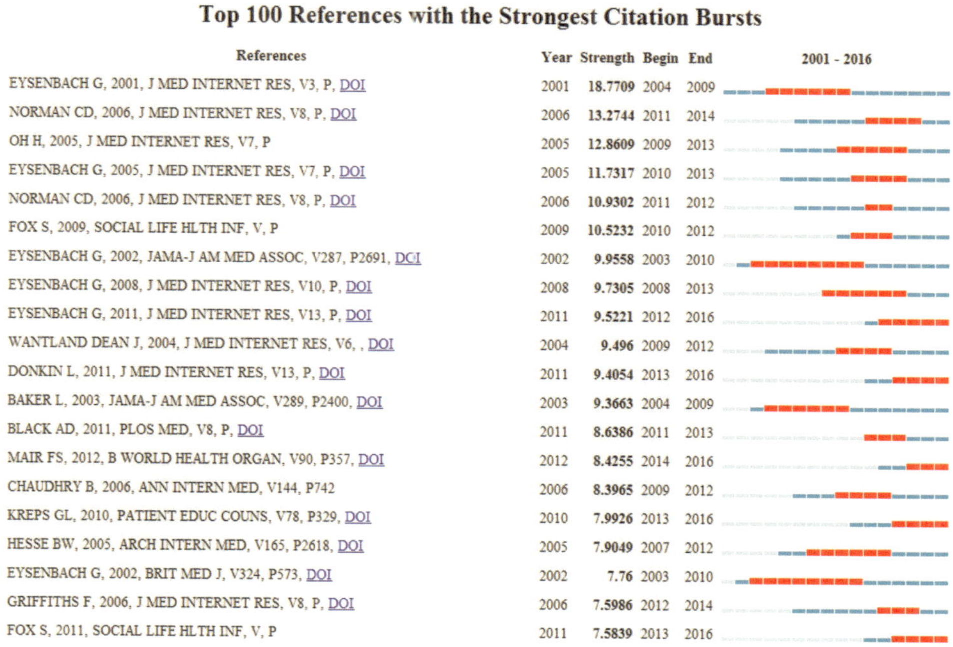

Figure 9.
Document co-citation bursting statistical chart.

The red part of the document is the period when cited rate raised most rapidly. At this stage, literature based on these knowledge bases is a research frontier. Drawing keywords co-occurrence network map combined with these citing articles can help identify research frontier.

Figure 8 shows the results of literature whose mutation time has been covered at least in the past 3 years and three documents were chosen which have the highest intensity of mutation (**Table 6**). Then we retrieved Web of Science for citing articles and conducted keyword cluster analysis and word frequency statistics. Combined with automatic identification function, we drew a cluster map of article citations, interpreted three key documents' citing document clustering and word frequency comprehensively, and did qualitative analysis of E-health academic field frontier research.

"A holistic framework to improve the uptake and impact of E-health technologies" is an article published by van Gemert-Pijinen Pewc in 2011. He found that a lot of E-health technologies were not appropriate for health services, the effect of which did not match people's expectation. After careful study, he believed that it was because developers ignored the dependencies among technologies, human characteristics, and environmental impact. Thus, he proposed a frame based on many scholars' studies to improve the quality of health services. Under such unity frame's guidance, E-health technology can be combined with the health sector better, but it needs more empirical support [18].

Based on high-frequency statistics and keyword co-occurrence cluster time-zone views (**Figure 10**), we can find high-frequency keywords including "intervention," "randomized controlled trial," "technology," "framework," "physical activity," and "self-management." Researchers use different research methods to compare the actual effects of E-health and then make reasonable predictions about the future of these applications, such as Van's framework [8]. Then the cost of applying emerging technologies in the medical field is reduced. Using a reasonable evaluation

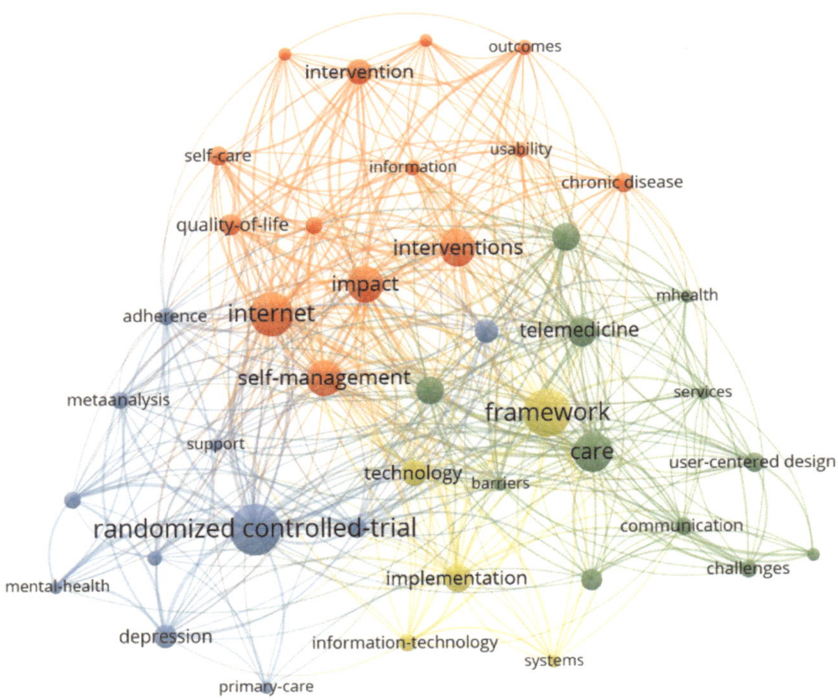

Figure 10.
Keyword-based clustering co-occurrence patterns.

framework to study the cost–benefit of Internet technology in the medical field has become a trend in the future.

Emergent literature of the cluster is "A systematic review of the impact of adherence on the effectiveness of e-therapies." This article reviewed the development of electronic treatment and the impact patient compliance has on treatment effect. It assessed factors that affect patient compliance and listed ways to improve electronic treatment and then concluded that electronic treatment was lacking in effective treatment of electronic protocols. Due to remote treatment, the patient was easier to be influenced by external factors. Further studies are needed to establish consensus compliance measurement program and understand the factors affected by compliance.

According to the high-frequency keywords and keyword co-occurrence clustering results (**Figure 11**), we can find high-frequency keywords named "randomized controlled trial," "adherence," "Internet," "depression," "intervention," "mental health," and "stress management." Scholars have studied methods to enhance patient attachment and loyalty to E-health technologies, including the use of network health technologies and mobile technology to manage the patient's physical and mental health, by increasing the degree of interaction between patients and electronic health technology to improve the patient's sense of e-therapy. In other words, making patients trust in e-therapy is a problem that needed to be solved.

"Factors that promote or inhibit the implementation of E-health system: an explanatory systematic review" is an article aimed to review the literature on the implementation of E-health to identify barriers and facilitators to E-health implementation and outstanding gaps in research on the subject. Mair published this review, and he found some interesting results: (1) work directed at making sense of E-health systems, specifying their purposes and benefits, establishing their value to users, and planning their implementation, (2) factors promoting or inhibiting engagement and participation, (3) effects on roles and responsibilities, (4) risk management, and (5) ways in which implementation processes might be reconfigured by user-produced knowledge [68]. He thought the published literature

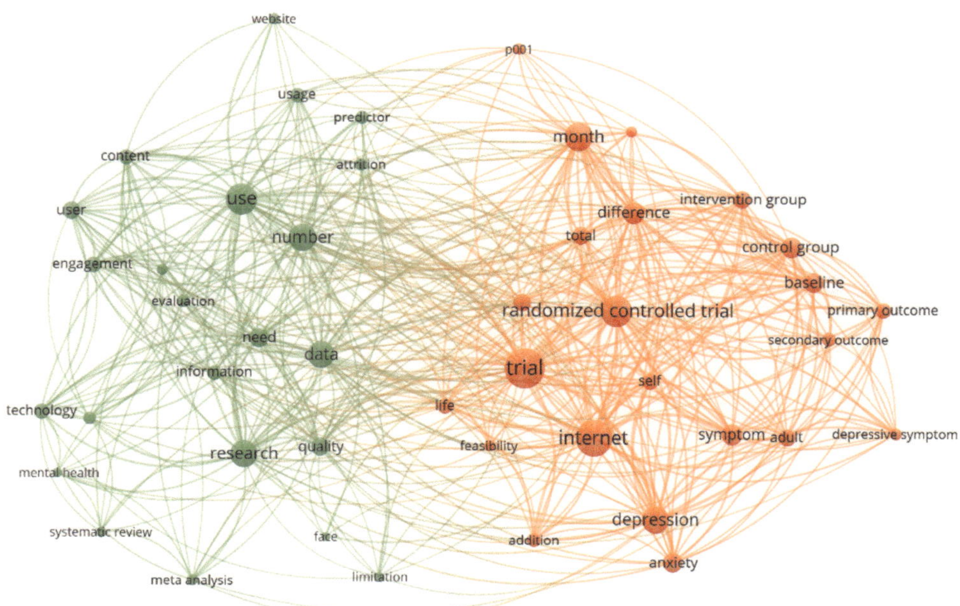

Figure 11.
Keyword-based clustering co-occurrence patterns.

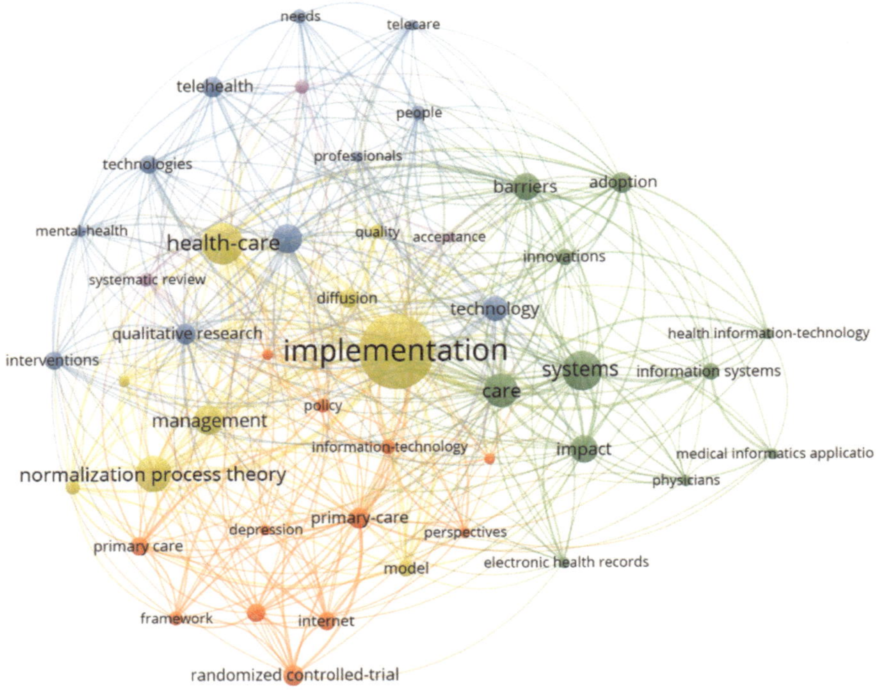

Figure 12.
Keyword-based clustering co-occurrence patterns.

focused on organizational issues and neglected the wider social framework which must be considered when introducing modern technologies.

Implementation, system, healthcare, normalization process theory, qualitative research, meaningful use, and impact are high-frequency keywords. The scholars who cite the article are concerned about the role and responsibility of electronic health in the medical process, risk management, ways to engage with professions, and how to ensure the potential benefits of new technologies (**Figure 12**). Mcevoy Rachel studies using the normalization process theory to research implementation process [69]. Deborah studies the role of digital technologies in self-management [70]. Jane does an organizational analysis of the implementation of telehealth in view of whole systems [71]. Scholars are also concerned about factors having impact on E-health applications, whether they are positive factors or obstacles [72–74]. With the increase of E-health project numbers, these areas deserved more empirical investigation and have been research frontiers, such as the ways to identify and anticipate how E-health services will impact everyday clinical practice, how new E-health services will affect clinical interactions and performance of clinical work, and the effects of different methods of engaging with professionals before and during the implementation of E-health.

3.4 Themes that develop quickly and need to be focused

Combined with literature review, among the research frontiers, E-health business is the core which is based on other articles concerned on commercialization of E-health which is experiencing explosive growth. As it goes, scholars proposed a lot of interesting and innovative project, attracting attention from the government and some companies. It seems that E-health is more cost-effective, efficient, and more convenient, which will substitute the face-to-face treatment in the future. However, although many of us think E-health is better than traditional treatment methods, governments operating E-health system decreased in number [75]. In view of that, we seek evidence that could help us find the reason. Since research about E-health has come into a new stage, technologies have already reached the demand, and governments are also positive that designing a complete E-health system is a top priority. Unfortunately, no one has satisfied the requirement [76]. A sustainable system need to be operated for a long time, so we need to take cost and profit into consideration. But we found that most of the research or surveys neglected these and they just concentrated on realizing E-health system [77–79]. On this occasion, how to reduce cost and profit will be the center of most scholars' study.

4. Discussion and conclusion

The E-health has been one of continued research focuses on the study of many academics, and the majority of scholars tended to publish papers to show their achievements. Annually published papers have reached 900 in 2015 and 2016, which is a pretty substantial number.

There was a gap between China and some developed countries in the researches of E-health. For instance, the USA, the UK, and Australia were the top three countries that published many articles. The impact of the UK was bigger than the USA according to the centrality index. The published quantity of references in China was not up to 1/6 of the USA and 1/3 of the UK. The time when China became to have centrality was 2004 which was later than most developed countries.

There were many institutions and authors working on this field. Among them, the number of authors who published at least one paper was 3770. On the one hand, it indicated that many scholars paid attention to E-health research from 2001 to 2016. On the other hand, there was great potential to improve the cooperation of authors, because the present relationships were not close which was revealed from the visualization map. Therefore, it is important to improve the allocation ability of resources and form cooperation network, so that we can deepen and improve the development of E-health.

Global E-health research focused on five topics ("Internet technology," "telemedicine," "E-health intervention on healthcare," "health system," and "personal health management"). With the development of information technology, E-health has been absorbing and applying emerging information technologies and applications. Among them, the application of the sophisticated cloud computing technology and big data are typical examples. Cloud computing is an emerging technology for Internet and composed of cluster of computers working upon distributed system that provide service in real time over a network. According to the definition by NIST, cloud computing is "a model that can provide distributed, rapidly provisioned and configurable computing resources" [78, 79]. Big Data in healthcare is concerned with meaningful datasets that are too large, too fast, and too complex for healthcare providers to process and interpret with existing tools. The application of big data technology can help solve the problem that medical field data is volume, various, and it grows too rapidly to deal with.

In addition, E-health has been a research focus of many counties over the world early in the twenty-first century. In detail, Internet, telemedicine, and health care became the focus in 2006. However, m-health, system management, and experimental intervention began to form the new study hot-spots, especially the commercialization of E-health from 2011. Therefore, scholars tended to set up a new E-health system so that we can improve the efficiency of health care and monitor people's health level in the distance and profit by developing E-health business.

This book chapter provides a reference for scholars working on this field and lays a foundation for further research on health IT policy.

5. Limitations

Although findings are based on the above analysis, there are still several potential limitations that may encourage further research efforts. First, this study only focuses on literature indexed by WoS and PubMed. Although WoS emphases paper quality to ensure accurate and meaningful data, it leads to some articles related to E-health not being covered. These will have some impact on the accuracy of research output on E-health.

Author details

Zhiyong Liu[1*†], Jianjun Su[2†] and Lei Ji[1]

1 School of Medicine and Health Management, Tongji Medical College, Huazhong University of Science and Technology, Wuhan City, Hubei Province, China

2 Futian District Maternal and Child Health Hospital, Shenzhen, China

*Address all correspondence to: zhiyongliu@hust.edu.cn

† These authors contributed equally.

References

[1] Wicks P, Stamford J, Grootenhuis MA, Haverman L, Ahmed S. Innovations in e-health. Quality of Life Research. 2014;**23**(1): 195-203. PMID: 23852096

[2] Stanberry B. Legal and ethical challenges of telemedicine and e-health. Proceedings of SPIE - The International Society for Optical Engineering. 2002: 47-66. DOI: 10.1117/12.480629

[3] LaPlante C, Peng W. A systematic review of e-health interventions for physical activity: An analysis of study design, intervention characteristics, and outcomes. Telemedicine and e-Health. 2011;**17**(7):509-523. PMID: 21718092

[4] Linn AJ, Vervloet M, van Dijk L, Smit EG, Van Weert JC. Effects of eHealth interventions on medication adherence: A systematic review of the literature. Journal of Medical Internet Research. 2011;**13**(4):e103. PMID: 22138112

[5] Minichiello V, Rahman S, Dune T, Scott J, Dowsett G. E-health: Potential benefits and challenges in providing and accessing sexual health services. BMC Public Health. 2013;**13**(1):790. PMID: 23987137

[6] Mair FS, May C, O'Donnell C, Finch T, Sullivan F, Murray E. Factors that promote or inhibit the implementation of e-health systems: An explanatory systematic review. Bulletin of the World Health Organization. 2012; **90**(5):357-364. PMID: 22589569

[7] Eysenbach G. What is e-health? Journal of Medical Internet Research. 2001;**3**(2):e20. DOI: 10.2196/jmir.3.2.e20

[8] van Rooij T, Marsh S. EHealth: Past and future perspectives. Personalized Medicine. 2016;**13**(1):57-70. DOI: 10.2217/pme.15.40

[9] J. Mitchell. From Telehealth to E-health: The Unstoppable Rise of E-health, 1999. ISBN: 064275036X

[10] World Health Organization. Leveraging e-Health to Improve National Health Systems in the African Region. Available from: http://www.aho.afro.who.int/sites/default/files/ahm/reports/47/ahm-issue-14-leveraging-ehealth.pdf

[11] Neuhauser L, Kreps GL. Rethinking communication in the E-health era. Journal of Health Psychology. 2003; **8**(1):7-23. PMID: 22113897

[12] Kwankam SY. What e-Health can offer. Bulletin of the World Health Organization. 2004;**82**(10):800-802. PMID: 15643805

[13] Anderer P, Gruber G, Parapatics S, Woertz M, Miazhynskaia T, Klosch G, et al. An E-health solution for automatic sleep classification according to Rechtschaffen and Kales: Validation study of the Somnolyzer 24 × 7 utilizing the Siesta database. Neuropsychobiology. 2005;**51**(3):115-133. PMID: 15838184

[14] Elkjaer M, Shuhaibar M, Burisch J, Bailey Y, Scherfig H, Laugesen B, et al. E-health empowers patients with ulcerative colitis: A randomised controlled trial of the web-guided 'Constant-care' approach. Gut. 2010;**59**(12):1652-1661. PMID: 21071584

[15] Ford DV, Jones KH, Verplancke JP, Lyons RA, John G, Brown G, et al. The Sail Databank: Building a national architecture for e-health research and evaluation. BMC Health Services Research. 2009;**9**(1):1-12. PMID: 19732426

[16] European Commission. eHealth Action Plan 2012–2020, 2012

[17] The Office of the National Coordinator for Health Information Technology. Federal Health IT Strategic Plan 2015–2020

[18] Royal College of Surgeons. Health and Social Care Act 2012. 2012.

[19] Dominguez-Mayo FJ, Escalona MJ, Mejias M, Aragon G, Garcia-Garcia JA, Torres J, et al. A strategic study about quality characteristics in e-health systems based on a systematic literature review. The Scientific World Journal. 2015;**2015**(4):1-11. PMID: 26146656

[20] Lee MH, Wu HC, Lin JY, Tan TH, Chan PC, Chen YF. Development and evaluation of an E-health system to care for patients with bladder pain syndrome/interstitial cystitis. International Journal of Urology. 2014; **21**(SI):62-68. PMID: 24807502

[21] Thompson HJ, Demiris G, Rue T, Shatil E, Wilamowska K, Zaslavsky O, et al. A Holistic approach to assess older adults' wellness using e-health technologies. Telemedicine and e-Health. 2011;**17**(10):794-800. PMID: 22011052

[22] de Veer A, Peeters JM, Brabers A, Schellevis FG, Rademakers J, Francke AL. Determinants of the intention to use e-Health by community dwelling older people. BMC Health Services Research. 2015;**15**(1):103. PMID: 25889884

[23] Hage E, Roo JP, van Offenbeek M, Boonstra A. Implementation factors and their effect on e-Health service adoption in rural communities: a systematic literature review. BMC Health Services Research. 2013;**13**(1):19. PMID: 23311452

[24] Currie WL, Seddon JJM. A cross-national analysis of eHealth in the European Union: Some policy and research directions. Information and Management-Amsterdam. 2014;**51**(6): 783-797. DOI: 10.1016/j.im.2014.04.004

[25] Fiordelli M, Diviani N, Schulz PJ. Mapping mHealth research: A decade of evolution. Journal of Medical Internet Research. 2013;**15**(5):e95. PMID: 23697600

[26] Kim HE, Jiang XQ, Kim J, Ohno-Machado L. Trends in biomedical informatics: Most cited topics from recent years. Journal of the American Medical Informatics Association - JAMIA. 2011;**18**(1):I166-I170. PMID: 22180873

[27] Chaomei C. Science mapping: A systematic review of the literature. Journal of Data and Information Science. 2017;**2**:1-40. DOI: 10.1515/jdis-2017-0006

[28] Sullivan B. The craft of information visualization: Readings and reflections. Technical Communication. 2004;**51**(1): 139-141

[29] Chen CM. CiteSpace II: Detecting and visualizing emerging trends and transient patterns in scientific literature. Journal of the China Society for Scientific & Technical Information. 2006;**57**(3):359-377. DOI: 10.1002/asi.20317

[30] Tho SW, Yeung YY, Wei R, Chan KW, So WW. A systematic review of remote laboratory work in science education with the support of visualizing its structure through the HistCite and CiteSpace software. International Journal of Science and Mathematics Education. 2017;**15**(7): 1217-1236. DOI: 10.1007/s10763-016-9740-z

[31] Xiao F, Li C, Sun J, Zhang L. Knowledge domain and emerging trends in organic photovoltaic technology: A scientometric review based on CiteSpace analysis. Frontiers in Chemistry. 2017;**5**. PMID: 28966923

[32] Webb TL, Joseph J, Yardley L, Michie S. Using the internet to promote health behavior change: A systematic review and meta-analysis of the impact of theoretical basis, use of behavior change techniques, and mode of delivery on efficacy. Journal of Medical Internet Research. 2010;**12**(1): e4. DOI: 10.2196/jmir.1376

[33] Blobel B, Roger-France F. A systematic approach for analysis and design of secure health information systems. International Journal of Medical Informatics. 2001;**62**(1):51-78. PMID: 11340006

[34] Blobel B. Authorisation and access control for electronic health record systems. International Journal of Medical Informatics. 2004;**73**(3): 251-257

[35] Blobel B, Pharow P. Security and privacy issues of personal health. In: 4th Conference of the International-Council-on-Medical-and-Care-Compunetics; Amsterdam, Netherlands; 2007. pp. 288-297. PMID: 15066555

[36] Schreier G, Kollmann A, Kramer M, Messmer J, Hochgatterer A, Kastner P. Mobile phone based user interface concept for health data acquisition at home. In: 9th International Conference on Computers Helping People with Special Needs; Paris, France; 2004. pp. 29-36. DOI: 10.1007/978-3-540-27817-7_5

[37] Schreier G, Eckmann H, Hayn D, Kreiner K, Kastner P, Lovell N. Web versus App—Compliance of patients in a telehealth diabetes management programme using two different technologies. Journal of Telemedicine and Telecare. 2012;**18**(8):476-480. PMID: 23209270

[38] Rodrigues J, Neves P. A survey on IP-based wireless sensor network solutions. International Journal of Communication Systems. 2010;**23**(8): 963-981. DOI: 10.1002/dac.1099

[39] Rodrigues J, Pereira O, Neves P. Biofeedback data visualization for body sensor networks. Journal of Network and Computer Applications. 2011;**34**(1): 151-158. DOI: 10.1016/j.jnca.2010.08.005

[40] Diallo O, Rodrigues J, Sene M, Xia F. Real-time query processing optimisation for wireless sensor networks. International Journal of Sensor Networks. 2015;**18**(1–2):49-61. DOI: 10.1016/j.ins.2014.03.081

[41] Gustafson DH, Hawkins RP, Boberg EW, McTavish F, Owens B, Wise M, et al. CHESS: 10 years of research and development in consumer health informatics for broad populations, including the underserved. Studies in Health Technology and Informatics. 2001;**65**(3):169-177. PMID: 12414016

[42] Eysenbach G. Consort-ehealth: Improving and standardizing evaluation reports of Web-based and mobile health interventions. Journal of Medical Internet Research. 2011;**13**(4):e126. PMID: 22209829

[43] Eysenbach G, Powell J, Kuss O, Sa ER. Empirical studies assessing the quality of health information for consumers on the world wide web: A systematic review. JAMA: The Journal of the American Medical Association. 2002;**287**(20):2691-2700. PMID: 12020305

[44] Eysenbach G, Kohler C. How do consumers search for and appraise health information on the world wide web? Qualitative study using focus groups, usability tests, and in-depth interviews. British Medical Journal. 2002;**324**(7337):573-577. PMID: 11884321

[45] Koch S. Home telehealth: Current state and future trends. International

Journal of Medical Informatics. 2006; **75**(8):565-576. PMID: 16298545

[46] Hilty DM, Ferrer DC, Parish MB, Johnston B, Callahan EJ, Yellowlees PM. The effectiveness of telemental health: A 2013 review. Telemedicine and e-Health. 2013;**19**(6):444-454. PMID: 16298545

[47] Andreassen HK, Bujnowska-Fedak MM, Chronaki CE, Dumitru RC, Pudule I, Santana S, et al. European citizens' use of E-health services: A study of seven countries. BMC Public Health. 2007;**7**(1):53. PMID: 17425798

[48] Beldad A, de Jong M, Steehouder M. How shall I trust the faceless and the intangible? A literature review on the antecedents of online trust. Computers in Human Behavior. 2010;**26**(5): 857-869. DOI: 10.1016/j.chb.2010.03.013

[49] Delaia CR, Freire IM. Subsidies to a policy information management of Embrapa soil based on regime of information. Perspectivas em Ciência da Informação. 2010;**15**(3):107-130. DOI: 10.1590/S1413-99362010000300007

[50] Berland GK, Elliott MN, Morales LS, Algazy JI, Kravitz RL, Broder MS, et al. Health information on the Internet: Accessibility, quality, and readability in English and Spanish. JAMA : The Journal of the American Medical Association. 2001;**285**(20):2612-2621. PMID: 11368735

[51] Gustafson DH, Hawkins R, Boberg E, Pingree S, Serlin RE, Graziano F, et al. Impact of a patient-centered, computer-based health information/support system. American Journal of Preventive Medicine. 1999; **16**(1):1-9. PMID: 9894548

[52] Baker L, Wagner TH, Singer S, Bundorf MK. Use of the Internet and e-mail for health care information: Results from a national survey. JAMA: The Journal of the American Medical Association. 2003;**289**(18):2400-2406. PMID: 12746364

[53] Hillestad R, Bigelow J, Bower A, Girosi F, Meili R, Scoville R, et al. Can electronic medical record systems transform health care? Potential health benefits, savings, and costs. Health Affairs. 2005;**24**(5):1103-1117. PMID: 16162551

[54] Eysenbach G. Medicine 2.0: Social networking, collaboration, participation, apomediation, and openness. Journal of Medical Internet Research. 2008;**10**(3):e22. DOI: 10.2196/jmir.1030

[55] Wantland DJ, Portillo CJ, Holzemer WL, Slaughter R, McGhee EM. The effectiveness of Web-based vs. non-Web-based interventions: A meta-analysis of behavioral change outcomes. Journal of Medical Internet Research. 2004;**6**(4):67-84. PMID: 15631964

[56] Eysenbach G. The law of attrition. Journal of Medical Internet Research. 2005;7(1). PMID: 15829473

[57] Lau A, Arguel A, Dennis S, Liaw ST, Coiera E. "Why Didn't it Work?" lessons from a randomized controlled trial of a web-based personally controlled health management system for adults with asthma. Journal of Medical Internet Research. 2015;**17**(12): e283. PMID: 26678294

[58] van Gemert-Pijnen J, Nijland N, van Limburg M, Ossebaard HC, Kelders SM, Eysenbach G, et al. A holistic framework to improve the uptake and impact of eHealth technologies. Journal of Medical Internet Research. 2011;**13**(4):2854-2866. PMID: 22155738

[59] Niyato D, Hossain E, Diamond J. IEEE 802.16/WiMax-based broadband wireless access and its application for

telemedicine/E-health services. IEEE Wireless Communications. 2007;**14**(1): 72-83. DOI: 10.1109/MWC.2007.314553

[60] Choi NG, DiNitto DM. The digital divide among low-income homebound older adults: Internet use patterns, eHealth literacy, and attitudes toward computer/internet use. Journal of Medical Internet Research. 2013;**15**(5): e93. PMID: 23639979

[61] Mohr DC, Schueller SM, Montague E, Burns MN, Rashidi P. The behavioral intervention technology model: An integrated conceptual and technological framework for eHealth and mHealth interventions. Journal of Medical Internet Research. 2014;**16**(6): e146. PMID: 24905070

[62] Fernandez-Cardenosa G, de la Torre-Diez I, Lopez-Coronado M, Rodrigues J. Analysis of cloud-based solutions on EHRs systems in different scenarios. Journal of Medical Systems. 2012;**36**(6):3777-3782. PMID: 22492177

[63] Kotwal PA, Singh AR. Evolution and effects of mobile cloud computing, middleware services on cloud, future prospects: A peek into the mobile cloud operating systems. In: 3rd IEEE International Conference on Computational Intelligence and Computing Research (ICCIC); Tamilnadu College of Engineering, Coimbatore, India; 2012. pp. 279-283. DOI: 10.1109/ICCIC.2012.6510270

[64] Shiji C. Survey of approaches to research front detection. New Technology of Library and Information Service. 2009;**25**(9):28-33. DOI: 10.11925/infotech.1003-3513.2009.09.05

[65] Chaomei C. The structure and dynamics of co-citation clusters: A multiple-perspective co-citation analysis. Journal of the Association for Information Science and Technology. 2010;**61**(7):1386-1409. DOI: 10.1002/asi.21309

[66] McEvoy R, Ballini L, Maltoni S, O'Donnell CA, Mair FS, MacFarlane A. A qualitative systematic review of studies using the normalization process theory to research implementation processes. Implementation Science. 2014;**9**(1):2. PMID: 24383661

[67] Morrison D, Wyke S, Agur K, Cameron EJ, Docking RI, MacKenzie AM, et al. Digital asthma self-management interventions: A systematic review. Journal of Medical Internet Research. 2014;**16**(2):e51. DOI: 10.2196/jmir.2814

[68] Hendy J, Chrysanthaki T, Barlow J, Knapp M, Rogers A, Sanders C, et al. An organisational analysis of the implementation of telecare and telehealth: The whole systems demonstrator. BMC Health Services Research. 2012;**12**(1):403. PMID: 23153014

[69] Lund S, Richardson A, May C. Barriers to advance care planning at the end of life: An explanatory systematic review of implementation studies. PLoS One. 2015;**10**(2):e116629. PMID: 25679395

[70] Wade VA, Eliott JA, Hiller JE. Clinician acceptance is the key factor for sustainable telehealth services. Qualitative Health Research. 2014; **24**(5):682-694. PMID: 24685708

[71] Kadu MK, Stolee P. Facilitators and barriers of implementing the chronic care model in primary care: A systematic review. BMC Family Practice. 2015;**16**(1):12. PMID: 25655401

[72] Tsuji M. Analysis of the long-run effect of e-health intervention on chronic diseases: A DID-PSM approach. In: 17th International Conference on E-health Networking, Application & Services (HealthCom); Boston, MA;

2015. pp. 511-516. DOI: 10.1109/HealthCom.2015.7454556

[73] Metler TAEM. What is the business model behind e-health? A pattern-based approach to sustainable profit (accepted). In: ECIS 2012 Proceedings; 2012. Available from: https://aisel.aisnet.org/ecis2012/61

[74] Leon MC, Nieto-Hipolito JI, Garibaldi-Beltran J, Amaya-Parra G, Luque-Morales P, Magana-Espinoza P, et al. Designing a model of a digital ecosystem for healthcare and wellness using the business model canvas. Journal of Medical Systems. 2016;**40**(6):1-9. PMID: 27118010

[75] Andreu-Perez J, Poon CCY, Merrifield RD, Wong STC, Yang G. Big data for health. IEEE Journal of Biomedical and Health Informatics. 2015;**19**(4):1193-1208. PMID: 26173222

[76] Grunwell D, Sahama T. Information accountability and health big data analytics: A consent-based model. In: 17th International Conference on E-health Networking, Application & Services (HealthCom); Boston, MA; 2015. pp. 195-199. DOI: 10.1109/HealthCom.2015.7454497

[77] Nachbagauer A, Dorda W, Duftschmid G, Holzer K, Janzek-Hawlat S, Strasser N, et al. Legal framework for secondary use medical data. In: Conference on eHealth—Health Informatics Meets eHealth; Vienna, Austria; 2013. pp. 143-148. PMID: 20461283

[78] Mell P, Grance T. The NIST definition of cloud computing. National Institute of Standards and Technology. 2009;**53**(6):50

[79] Hu Y, Bai G. A systematic literature review of cloud computing in ehealth. Health Informatics-An International Journal (HIIJ). November 2014;**3**(4). DOI: 10.5121/hiij.2014.3402

Section 3

Scientific Collaboration and Citation Analysis

Chapter 5

Contrasting High Scientific Production with Low International Collaboration and Scientific Impact: The Brazilian Case

Cristina Haeffner, Sonia Regina Zanotto, Helena B. Nader and Jorge Almeida Guimarães

Abstract

The article presents an analysis of scientific production and impact among 35 most productive countries in the world. In the period 2000–2016, these countries produced 92% of the world publications. A correlation of international collaboration and scientific impact is shown. Differently from this pattern, Brazil shows high quantitative performance but low scientific impact, which is attributed to its low level of international collaboration. By contrast, instead of a generalized cooperation, as many undeveloped countries do, Brazil uses its internal effort to explore cooperation in a more symmetrical manner. Thus, in several areas, Brazil occupies a prominent position, including technological sectors, enabling it to occupy the eighth world's economy position. The data confirm that an efficient internal scientific effort combined with well-balanced international cooperation can be more effective to enable countries to achieve higher levels of development in order to meet their technical and socioeconomic challenges. Brazil was able to reach the first step but did not follow the same track concerning higher scientific impact.

Keywords: scientometric analysis, international scientific collaboration, impact, BRICS, Latin American countries

1. Introduction

Collaboration is irreversibly present in scientific practice. The idea that collaboration contributes to increase scientific productivity has already been addressed at national and international levels. It can be said that collaboration is a phenomenon accepted by the scientific community and stimulated by development agencies, as emphasized by Katz and Martin [1]. In fact, international scientific collaboration network has been growing even fast in recent years [2, 3]. This practice occurs in the social context of individual behavior, and it is, therefore, a complex phenomenon defined as the interaction between two or more groups of scientists, which provides the sharing of activities in the sense of achieving common goals [4].

Scientific collaboration can also show negative aspects when, for instance, collaboration occurs among researchers in an unethical manner as for the case of animals and even human tests made in less developed countries, since this type of experiment is prohibited in advanced countries. Collaboration can also exert a "lobbying" power by influencing political decisions for the release of funds, benefiting only some groups to the detriment of others working on the same theme [4]. The author emphasizes, however, that the final stage of a successful collaboration is co-authoring articles, because the dissemination of results through scientific publication is, in fact, the traditional result of research. Furthermore, international collaboration feeds other studies and new projects, which strengthen scientific communities. In addition, the publication is a proof of the good utilization of the financial resources used in research that generate new knowledge.

The productivity of Brazilian science, including aspects of international scientific collaboration, has been studied by several authors. Some years ago, Leta and Chaimovich [5] carried out a study on the size of Brazilian production in relation to the rest of the world, covering the period 1981–2000. The researchers showed that in the period studied, the countries that had more scientific collaboration with Brazil were from Europe and North America. While, with the United States, such collaboration reached 40.5%, the number of collaborative publications with Latin American countries represented less than 10%. The data indicate, for that time, the trend that in developing countries, collaboration tended to be more intense with more developed countries. It was also clear that international collaboration benefited the production and visibility of publications from lesser developed countries. Glänzel and Schubert [6] revealed some facets of scientific collaboration including Brazilian data. According to the authors, collaboration in domestic co-authorship is clearly influenced by two factors: (i) the size of the scientific community in the country (evidenced in the scientific production of the United States and the United Kingdom), since in these countries it is easier for a researcher to find scientific partners than for researchers working in a small country, and (ii) cultural reasons, such as geography, language, politics, or comparative advantage. However, the authors point out some situations which are not included in these rules, as is the case in some typically international countries that conduct research with high level of scientific domesticity (such as Hungary in agriculture and environment or the Czech Republic in neuroscience and behavior). Conversely, there are other cases where a large country is low in scientific domesticity (e.g., China in the areas of agriculture and the environment) [6].

Other aspects of scientific collaboration raised by Vanz [7] and Vanz and Stumpf [8] show that in Brazilian research, as in other countries, collaboration promotes access to equipment and materials, allowing sharing of scientific knowledge and greater specialization of research groups. In addition, they affirm that the results of a published work in co-authorship are more likely to be accepted and obtain a greater number of citations when compared to works published individually. The authors also point out that good communication between researchers, sharing of social skills, and the ability to conduct teamwork are fundamental characteristics for the success of scientific collaboration, especially when it involves geographical distances and needs of a better understanding of concepts and methodologies and when collaboration involves researchers from different areas [8]. Santin, Vanz, and Stumpf [9] point out the predominance of bilateral collaboration in the Brazilian production of articles in Evolutionary Biology published in the period 2004–2006. Though using old data, it should be noted that the authors selected one of the few areas in which Brazil has the highest index of international collaboration. As a fairly new area in the world scientific scenario, Evolutionary Biology attracts a high level of international cooperative research. In this specific case, most of the articles resulting from Brazilian researchers had the participation of co-authors from some other countries. The authors point out that 47% of the Brazilian publications in this field included researchers from the United States, United Kingdom, France, and

Germany, while only 5% were from Argentina. The data indicate the preference for international collaboration with developed countries, thus not only confirming the findings shown by Leta and Chaimovich [5] but also revealing that collaboration with neighboring countries, such as Argentina, is practically negligible.

The above studies do not include cases of "naturally forced" cooperation driven by the necessity to enable mutual technological advances between more developed countries and even competitors in the field of innovation. Furthermore, the issue of international collaboration has not been addressed for other factors exerting attraction for collaboration. For example, in Brazil, the possibility of making domestic science is more visible, such as in the areas of biodiversity and tropical medicine, agriculture, biotechnology, and bioeconomy, which are research fields with a strong attractiveness for international collaborators. Contrarily, in this sense, Brazil is a typical case where Brazilian scientists cite more than they are cited. In fact, the feature of low quotation between peers seems to permeate and constitutes a challenge for scientists not only in Brazil but throughout Latin America since long ago [10], which is still a reality today.

A comparison of the production and scientific collaboration of the countries of the BRICS group was made by Finardi [11] and Finardi and Buratti [12]. The studies highlighted the importance of international collaboration in the scientific production of these countries. The authors emphasize that the relationship between countries is strengthened not only in economic aspects but also in relation to the scientific partnerships. They firstly analyzed the intra-BRICS collaboration and compared the relative strength of relations between the member countries. Secondly, the authors sought to understand the pattern of collaboration of the BRICS countries in relation to that with other collaborative countries, regardless of the direction of the partnerships. The data showed that the intra-BRICS collaborations are weaker than the collaborations with the other countries studied. The results indicate that it would be relevant to plan policies aimed at promoting scientific collaboration among the five countries, such as fostering scientific research, and this is generally considered a strategic measure for a country's growth. Therefore, improving the level of collaboration among the five BRICS countries could make it possible to have positive effects on the social and economic development as desired by developing countries.

The finding that intra-BRICS collaboration, that is, collaboration between Brazil, Russia, India, China, and South Africa, has been shown to be weaker than with the rest of the world was also studied by Bouabid, Paul-Hus, and Larivière [3]. The authors studied the productivity evolution of the G7 member countries, formed by the United States, Germany, Canada, France, Italy, Japan, and United Kingdom, in relation to BRICS member countries. They compared production and scientific collaboration in fields employing high technologies such as engineering, medical sciences, earth sciences, and space sciences and found that the scientific activities of BRICS are reinforced by high-technology exports upon their collaboration with the G7 countries. While the high-technology exports made by most BRICS countries to the G7 countries increased over the period studied, compared to the flow of these exports among the BRICS countries, these collaborations remained very weak. By extension, it can be seen that the same phenomenon occurs with the scientific collaboration between the countries of Latin America. In other words, the scientific collaboration continues to be lower than the rates of collaboration with the most productive central countries. A study about collaboration and scientific impact of Latin American countries in the area of biotechnology found that the increase in research in this sector originates from international collaboration, especially with the more developed countries, those occupying the influential positions in the area, such as the United States, Japan, Germany, England, Spain, and France [13]. The authors emphasize that, in a network of scientific collaboration, it is not only important to have a good production and impact but to have the capacity to become a mediator or link in establishing collaboration between the countries participating in the productive research network. In this way, the research groups from the less developed countries that make this communication bridge increase their capacities to absorb resources have access to new technologies and resources at high-technology laboratories, thus increasing the quality of their results. The observations derived from the studies with BRICS and Latin American countries were confirmed in our work with actualized data showing, once again, that either for historical, cultural, or economic reasons, scientific collaboration and consequently the development of the member countries of these groups will not occur as a result of intragroup collaboration, but instead, mainly with the most productive countries. Furthermore, despite the recognized advantages of international cooperation, we have shown in a previous article [14] that countries that have not prepared themselves to exploit the opportunities offered by international collaboration do not internalize these advantages for their own best technical-scientific and economic benefit.

As compared to previous studies, in the present work, we explore several new aspects, including (i) a much longer and recent studied period, (ii) the evolution of Brazilian scientific productivity and of its most significant areas, (iii) correlation between the number of graduate programs and the number of research groups, and (iv) correlation between international collaboration and citation impact of the 35 countries with high scientific productivity. Thus, the aim of the present work is to demonstrate the influence of international collaboration on the scientific impact generated by the citations in four aspects: (a) in the comparison between the 35 most productive countries, a small group of countries (about 17% of the world countries listed in the ESI database), which includes Brazil, that produce 92% of the world publications; (b) comparing Brazil with the most productive Latin American countries; (c) the position of Brazil among the countries of the BRICS group (Brazil, Russia, India, China, and South Africa), and (d) contrasting Brazil's low international cooperation and consequent lower scientific impact with its recognized technological performance in several applied fields such as tropical agriculture, technology for exploiting petroleum resources in deep sea water, woodland recovery of once infertile land ("cerrados"), cellulose and paper mill industry, sophisticated bank automation, construction of alcohol-propelled motor vehicles, aircraft design, and industrial production, among others [15]. The study uses comparative analysis among the most productive countries. For this purpose, data were collected on the scientific performance of the countries in the 22 areas of the Essential Science Indicators (ESI), where all countries listed in the InCites database (Thomson Reuters 2016) are represented. It is important to note that the metrics used in InCites, although not frequently used in Brazil, are widely recognized for comparative studies. According to Bornmann and Leydesdorf [16] with InCites, it is possible to study the impact and the citation behavior of countries using a time window for a long period of publications, thus allowing to compare areas with normalized indicators in an efficient manner.

2. Methodology

The article results from a scientometric study through the analyses of bibliographic indicators extracted from recognized databases, described below. International collaboration and other indicators were obtained through the survey of InCites platform, a fully integrated Web of Science (WoS) database. This analytic tool is under the responsibility of former Thomson Reuters (now Clarivate Analytics), Philadelphia/USA, available through institutional subscription and internal access in the Coordenação de Aperfeiçoamento de Pessoal de Nível Superior (CAPES).

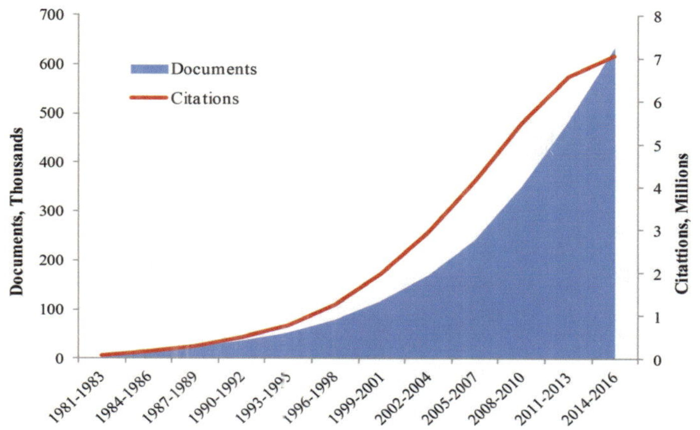

Figure 1.
Brazilian scientific production: accumulated number of articles and citations. Source: InCites dataset updated 2017-10-14. Includes Web of Science content indexed through 2017-10-3.

The InCites Platform is composed of several other databases. In this study, we selected the Essential Sciences Indicators (ESI), which classifies scientific production in 22 areas of knowledge. Bibliographical data in these areas of ESI include articles and reviews of the Science Citation Index Expanded and the Social Science Citation Index, but do not include the indexed papers of Arts and Humanities, Conference Proceedings Citation Index, and Book Citation Index. ESI is part of the InCites platform and a filter for large areas of knowledge, making it easier to compare them. Each journal that makes up the ESI database is classified in only one area, with no overlap of subjects, or double counting of articles between areas. When the journal is classified as multidisciplinary (as science or nature, for instance), the system makes a disambiguation of the theme of an article by the topics of the journals cited in this one, so if the article published in one of these journals refers to a certain theme, the references will confirm in which of the 22 areas the article in question will be indexed. Except for the accumulated data shown in **Figure 1** and **Table 1** where the numbers started in the trimester 1981–1983, the present study covered a period of 17 years (between 2000 and 2016). The data were downloaded and worked with Excel listing the following indicators:

1. Articles or documents: Number of published papers, including articles, full proceeding papers, and reviews.

2. Times cited: Number of citations received during the period.

3. % Documents cited: percentage of cited documents as a fraction of total documents in the period.

4. Citation impact: Average number of citations received by the publications (or area) in a given period. It is the result of the division of the total number of citations by the total number of publications in the period.

5. Impact relative to world (IRW): It concerns to the impact of an area or country relative to the world's average impact of that area or the average of all countries together. An IRW index greater than 1.0 indicates that impact in a specific area or country is larger than the average impact of all areas together and, in the case of countries, that the impact of a country is higher than the average of all countries [14].

6. International collaboration: Number of documents in international co-authoring.

7. Percentage of international collaboration: Proportion of documents published in international co-authoring in relation to the total number of publications.

No.	Areas	1981–1983			2014–2016			Growth number doc.
		N. doc.	IRW	% Doc. in top 1%	N. documents	IRW	% doc. in top 1%	
1	Agricultural sciences	700	0.294	0.6	13,181	0.517	0.6	17.8
2	Biology and biochemistry	550	0.724	0.0	7461	0.907	0.4	12.6
3	Chemistry	533	0.822	0.4	10,824	1.066	0.1	19.3
4	Clinical medicine	1811	0.344	0.4	33,287	0.846	1.1	17.4
5	Computer science	43	0.866	0.0	3169	0.581	0.5	72.7
6	Economics and business	42	1.155	0.0	1154	0.402	0.7	26.5
7	Engineering	189	0.589	0.5	7562	0.777	0.5	39.0
8	Environment/ecology	91	0.748	0.0	5804	1.152	1.3	62.8
9	Geosciences	185	0.905	0.5	2961	0.916	0.6	15.0
10	Immunology	86	1.680	0.0	3772	1.204	1.2	42.9
11	Materials science	38	0.475	2.6	4697	0.826	0.2	122.6
12	Mathematics	241	0.993	1.2	3179	0.398	0.4	12.2
13	Microbiology	82	1.401	0.0	2913	1.089	0.8	34.5
14	Molecular biology and genetics	184	0.949	0.0	4244	1.105	0.7	22.1
15	Multidisciplinary	282	0.066	0.7	232	0.931	1.3	−0.2
16	Neuroscience and behavior	100	1.790	1.0	5400	0.987	0.6	53.0
17	Pharmacology and toxicology	129	1.070	0.0	4990	0.765	0.5	37.7
18	Physics	723	1.210	0.6	8146	1.589	1.8	10.3
19	Plant and animal science	659	0.530	0.2	17,719	0.534	0.6	25.9
20	Psychiatry/psychology	115	0.214	0.0	2433	0.866	1.5	20.2
21	Social sciences, general	363	0.483	1.4	6837	0.381	0.7	17.8
22	Space science	109	1.429	0.0	1493	2.676	3.4	12.7
Brazil		**7255**	**0.649**	**0.4**	**149,787**	**0.862**	**0.8**	**19.6**

Comparison of the two distant triennials: 1981–1983 and 2014–2016. Source: exported date 2017-10-13. InCites dataset updated 2017-09-23. Includes Web of Science content indexed through 2017-07-31.

Table 1.
Growth of the Brazilian scientific production of all ESI areas.

3. Results and discussion

Despite its late entry into the world's science circle, in the last decades, Brazil has been experiencing extraordinary growth in the production of indexed scientific articles published in periodicals with international qualification. In the 1960s, the average of scientific publications published in periodicals indexed in the database of the former Institute for Scientific Information (ISI) was 52 scientific articles annually; in 1970 there were only 64 articles, representing 0.019% of world production, jumping to 10,555 complete articles in 2001 [17, 18]. At present (2012–2016), Brazil publishes on average ca. 50,000 articles per year. **Figure 1** shows the evolution of the Brazilian scientific production covering all the 12 trimesters (from 1981 to 1983 up to the present 2014–2016). The data report the accumulated growth of published articles as well as that of accumulated citations. The amount of documents published in the period accounts for a total of 636,000, while that of citations reached more than 7 million, which indicates an average of 11.1 citations per article (impact) for the whole period. This manner of representing the mean impact is thought by the authors to be more adequate than that commonly used (year by year) way because, as it is well known, citations of recent papers (less than 8–10 years) are small, resulting in a low index of the impact factor, a common feature applied to all fields and world science [19].

As seen in **Table 1**, except for the multidisciplinary field, an expressive growth is found in all research areas in Brazil. On average, between the first triennial (1981–1983) and the last one (2014–2016), there was a growth of 20-fold for the total number of articles, where some areas such as materials science (123-fold), computer science (73-fold), environment and ecology (63-fold), and neuroscience and behavior (53-fold) show much higher growth. It is also seen in the table that the other indicators, the impact relative to world (IRW), increased from 0.65 to 0.86 and the percentage of top 1% articles from 0.4 to 0.8%.

The evolution of Brazilian scientific production occurred within a period of only 35 years and allowed Brazil to be included, in 2009, among the top 20 scientifically most productive countries. This time period is coincident with that followed after the foundation of the Ministry of Science and Technology (MCT, today MCTIC) in 1985. The rapid development of scientific activities in Brazil was based on the establishment of a vigorous postgraduate program [15], which began in the late 1960s and resulted in the consolidation of the current 37,640 research groups registered in the country and covering all scientific areas [20]. **Figure 2** illustrates the recent growth of the Brazilian graduate programs, and **Figure 3** illustrates the evolution and consolidation of research groups. As it can be seen, there is a parallelism among the indicators of the three growth curves covering the period studied. This growth also correlates well with increasing

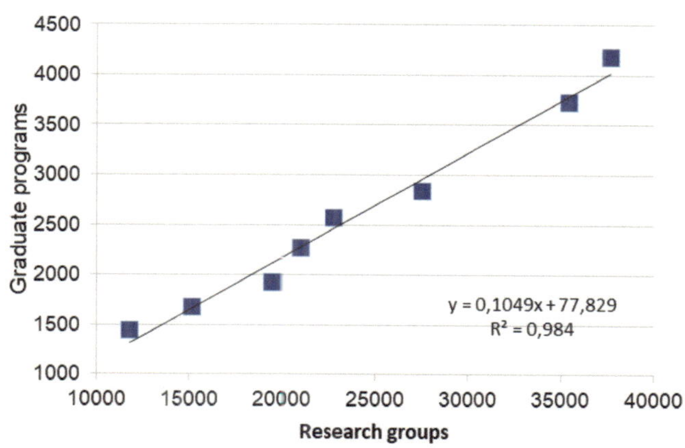

Figure 2.
Correlation between the number of graduate programs and the number of research groups in Brazil—2000–2016. Source: CAPES. Geocapes. http://geocapes.capes.gov.br/geocapes2/ and CNPq (2017). Estatísticas CNPq. http://estatico.cnpq.br/.

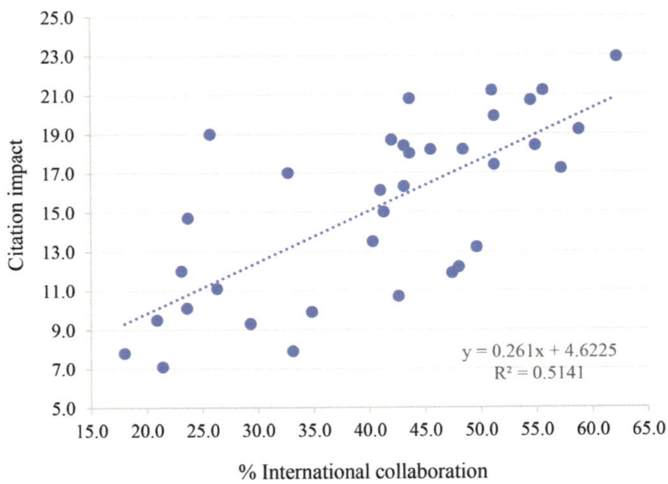

Figure 3.
Correlation between % international collaboration and citation impact of the 35 countries with high scientific productivity (2000–2016). Source: ESI-InCites dataset updated 2017-04-15. Includes Web of Science content indexed through 2017-02-03.

funding from the federal agencies CAPES, CNPq, and FINEP and especially with that of state agencies FAPESP, FAPEMIG, and FAPERJ in the period (data not shown). It was also positively influenced by the availability of The Portal of Periodicals by CAPES in 2001 [18].

In order to compare Brazil with other countries, in this study we also explore some characteristics of world scientific production in the period 2000–2016. **Table 1** lists the 35 countries with the largest number of articles in WoS, i.e., countries with a contribution of at least 0.5% of the world production which account for 92.2% of the world total scientific production in the period (**Table 2**). Brazil presently ranks 14th. While the table includes all BRICS countries, from Latin America only Brazil and Mexico appear. Other quantitative and qualitative bibliometric studies are also presented in **Table 2**. In the period 2000–2016, the world scientific production reached 26,103,636 articles, while the 35 most productive countries totaled 28,671,597 documents. This quantitative artifact is due to the phenomenon known as double counting [14, 18], which occurs, in this comparison, whenever the sum of publications is counted country by country, since articles with co-authorship including authors from two or more countries are counted at least twice. It was found in a previous study [14], covering the period 2011–2014, that double counting corresponded, in the period, to 33.1% of world production. Here, double counting of articles reaches 16.1% (**Table 2**). This discrepancy is due to the coverage for a longer period of years in the present article, since it is known that the indexes of international collaboration that affect double counting have been increasing in recent years. After correction, the total of articles in the 35 countries of **Table 1** corresponds, in the period, to 24,055,470 or 92.2% of the world total without double counting. Therefore, the data indicate that the countries in **Table 2**, which represent 17% of world countries, constitute an adequate sample for the present bibliometric study.

Table 2 also shows a high percentage of cited articles (average of 73.3%), with small individual variation: 65.9% (Russia) to 79.4% (Finland), all above the world average 66.5%. These indices are reflected in a high total of citations which in turn produces an average impact index of 16.3 which is 1.2 times higher than the world average index (13.5).

DOI: http://dx.doi.org/10.5772/intechopen.85825

Country	Rank	Articles	Times cited	% Doc. Cited	Citation impact	International collaborations	% International collaborations
United States	1	7,923,518	150,865,186	67.5	19.0	2,038,606	25.7
China	2	2,275,635	23,014,726	73.9	10.1	537,660	23.6
Germany	3	1,829,635	34,150,179	70.1	18.7	768,571	42.0
England	4	1,814,621	32,931,581	73.2	18.2	824,910	45.5
Japan	5	1,555,919	22,874,614	74.5	14.7	368,209	23.7
France	6	1,231,668	22,351,252	75.9	18.2	596,112	48.4
Canada	7	1,109,651	20,003,328	72.9	18.0	484,151	43.6
Italy	8	1,051,109	16,907,001	74.1	16.1	430,418	41.0
Spain	9	837,380	12,579,920	73.9	15.0	345,891	41.3
Australia	10	822,175	13,371,337	73.1	16.3	354,313	43.1
India	11	713,637	6,808,521	72.2	9.5	148,773	20.9
Korea	12	691,631	7,650,919	72.0	11.1	182,056	26.3
Netherlands	13	629,561	13,319,873	75.3	21.2	320,978	51.0
Brazil	14	539,049	4,997,160	69.5	9.3	158,083	29.3
Russia	15	510,662	4,039,770	65.9	7.9	168,817	33.1
Switzerland	16	448,485	10,283,870	76.1	22.9	279,150	62.2
Sweden	17	407,754	8,438,475	78.1	20.7	222,203	54.5
Taiwan	18	386,178	4,638,999	77.3	12.0	89,180	23.1
Turkey	19	378,817	2,963,670	65.9	7.8	68,318	18.0
Poland	20	353,032	3,498,064	70.7	9.9	122,718	34.8
Belgium	21	335,616	6,431,262	75.7	19.2	197,217	58.8
Scotland	22	266,900	5,541,755	73.7	20.8	116,315	43.6
Iran	23	259,961	1,834,821	68.7	7.1	55,688	21.4

Country	Rank	Articles	Times cited	% Doc. Cited	Citation impact	International collaborations	% International collaborations
Denmark	24	248,517	5,266,614	76.4	21.2	138,171	55.6
Israel	25	241,825	4,458,141	75.8	18.4	104,323	43.1
Austria	26	240,026	4,136,021	71.9	17.2	137,232	57.2
Greece	27	194,490	2,618,069	72.6	13.5	78,315	40.3
Finland	28	194,118	3,861,474	79.4	19.9	99,452	51.2
Hong Kong	29	180,864	3,077,238	79.0	17.0	59,202	32.7
Mexico	30	175,970	1,886,483	69.9	10.7	74,953	42.6
Portugal	31	175,260	2,317,498	71.7	13.2	86,924	49.6
Norway	32	175,131	3,224,102	77.7	18.4	96,192	54.9
Czech Republic	33	163,456	1,944,604	72.3	11.9	77,412	47.4
Singapore	34	162,098	2,818,900	77.7	17.4	83,015	51.2
South Africa	35	147,248	1,800,982	71.4	12.2	70,708	48.0
Total and average		**28,671,597**	**466,906,409**	**73.3**	**15.3**	**9,984,236**	**40.8**
World (without double counting)		**26,238,799**	**354,501,667**	**66.5**	**13.2**	—	**18.0**
World (with double counting)		**31,110,404**				Percent double counting: 16.1%	

Source: ESI-InCites dataset updated 2017-04-15. Includes Web of Science content indexed through 2017-02-03.

Table 2.
Scientific performance of the 35 most productive countries in 2000–2016.

On the other hand, it can be observed in the table that the robust quantitative data of the scientific production of the 35 countries conceal the dispersion of the most important qualitative components of this ranking: the scientific impact (Switzerland 22.9, Iran 7.1) and international collaboration (Switzerland, 62.2%, Turkey, 18.0%), with the average for the 35 countries of 15.3 and 40.8%, respectively, for the two indicators. It should be mentioned that when the data of the most recent year (2016) is taken, the international cooperation index of Switzerland increases from 62.2 to 72.1%, Turkey from 18.0 to 21.1%, and the average of the 35 countries from 40.8 to 49.9% (data not shown), thus confirming the recent tendency for the growth of international collaboration among countries. Analyzing the impact ranking (numbers in brackets in the column), a different figure is shown where the first ten countries in number of publications do not appear in a similar position in the impact ranking. Here, the first seven positions are occupied by Switzerland, Denmark, the Netherlands, Scotland, Sweden, Finland, and Belgium; none of them is present in the first quantitative positions, but all of them are showing a high proportion of international collaboration, thus indicating again the correlation—high international collaboration and higher citation impact—as shown in **Figure 3**.

Table 3 clearly illustrates the influence of international cooperation on the index of scientific impact of the countries. Here we can see that the 21 countries with the highest international collaboration rates (above the average of **Table 2**, or 40.8%), varying between 41.3% (Spain) and 62.2% (Switzerland), have an average impact well above the mean of all countries. In this group, only the United States (25.7%) and Hong Kong (32.7%) have international cooperation level below average. The average impact index of the 21 countries in this group is 17.9 and the international collaboration is 49.2%. On the other hand, among the 14 other countries with the lowest impact rates, only Mexico has international collaboration above the average of the 35 countries. In this second group, the average impact index of the 14 countries is 11.4 and the international collaboration is 28.3%. The indices of the countries in the first group are, respectively, 57 and 74% higher than those in the second group, confirming again this positive correlation: high international collaboration, higher citation impact. Brazil is located in the group of countries that cite more than they are cited [10]. As with most countries with a low level of international cooperation, Brazil's low impact index (9.3), one of the lowest among the 35 most productive countries, is, in turn, followed by a low percentage (29.3%) of international scientific collaboration, also of the lowest in the whole world.

This work also included comparative studies with countries in Latin America, some of them linked to the MERCOSUL agreement and the component countries of the BRICS group. Both consort of countries present common commercial and social interests including the perspective of presenting some level of scientific collaboration. The comparison of Brazil with other Latin American countries is shown in **Table 4** which presents the data of the scientific production of the 12 most productive countries of Latin America in the period 2000–2016. This group includes members of the MERCOSUL: Argentina, Brazil, Chile (associated), Uruguay, and Venezuela (suspended in 2016). The evolution of the percentage of international collaboration in the period studied for the five most productive countries in the region is shown in **Figure 4**. Taken in consideration the number of WoS indexed publications shown in **Table 4**, it is seen that Brazil alone responds for more than 50% of publications of the 12 countries. It is also seen that half of these countries produced in the large period analyzed a small number of publications having all of them a very high percentage (64.4–86.3%) of international collaboration. The average percentage of cited articles in the 12 countries (71.1%) is relatively high compared to the world, and this high value is in agreement with that of the scientific impact (13.3). The variation in international collaboration ranged from 29.3 to 86.3%, with a high

More than 41% of international collaboration					Less than 41% of international collaboration			
N.	Country	Citation impact	Rank	% International collaborations	Country	Citation impact	Rank	% International collaborations
1	Switzerland	22.9	1	62.2	United States	19.0	8	25.7
2	Denmark	21.2	2	55.6	Hong Kong	17.0	17	32.7
3	Netherlands	21.2	3	51.0	Japan	14.7	21	23.7
4	Scotland	20.8	4	43.6	Greece	13.5	22	40.3
5	Sweden	20.7	5	54.5	Taiwan	12.0	25	23.1
6	Finland	19.9	6	51.2	Korea	11.1	27	26.3
7	Belgium	19.2	7	58.8	Mexico	10.7	28	42.6
8	England	18.7	9	42.0	China	10.1	29	23.6
9	Israel	18.4	10	43.1	Poland	9.9	30	34.8
10	Norway	18.4	11	54.9	India	9.5	31	20.9
11	Germany	18.2	12	45.5	Brazil	9.3	32	29.3
12	France	18.2	13	48.4	Russia	7.9	33	33.1
13	Canada	18.0	14	43.6	Turkey	7.8	34	18.0
14	Singapore	17.4	15	51.2	Iran	7.1	35	21.4
15	Austria	17.2	16	57.2	—	—	—	—
16	Australia	16.3	18	43.1	—	—	—	—
17	Italy	16.1	19	41.0	—	—	—	—
18	Spain	15.0	20	41.3	—	—	—	—
19	Portugal	13.2	23	49.6	—	—	—	—
20	South Africa	12.2	24	48.0	—	—	—	—
21	Czech Republic	11.9	26	47.4	—	—	—	—
Average		**17.9**	—	**49.2**	**Average**	**11.4**	—	**28.3**

Source: ESI-InCites dataset updated 2017-04-15. Includes Web of Science content indexed through 2017-02-03.

Table 3.
Influence of the international collaboration on the scientific impact of countries: 2000–2016.

average rate (61.5%). Brazil, despite its higher production, has the lowest impact rate (9.3) and international collaboration (29.3%) level. Contrasting with their rate of publications, the countries with the highest impact rates also present the highest levels of international collaboration, confirming the observation that there is an intrinsic relationship between these two indicators. Thus, in comparison with the most productive Latin American countries, Brazil is behind the other countries of the group reinforcing the significant observation: greater proportion of international collaboration, higher index of scientific impact [14].

However, according to recent studies [14, 21], it is doubtful whether the apparently positive data of high scientific impact by itself with low autonomous significant science production and very high dependence of international collaboration would be able to give good perspectives for the country's social and economic development.

Country	Rank	Articles	Times cited	% Doc. cited	Citation impact	International collaborations	% International collaborations
Brazil	1	539,049	4,997,160	69.5	9.3	158,083	29.3
Mexico	2	175,970	1,886,433	69.9	10.7	74,953	42.6
Argentina	3	133,349	1,611,771	73.4	12.1	56,759	42.6
Chile	4	87,419	1,107,194	71.9	12.7	49,465	56.6
Colombia	5	42,021	417,829	64.3	9.9	25,034	59.6
Venezuela	6	21,667	239,514	68.2	11.1	11,064	51.1
Cuba	7	14,331	145,440	71.1	10.2	9231	64.4
Peru	8	12,892	181,816	66.6	14.1	10,246	79.5
Uruguay	9	11,920	158,319	73.5	13.3	7997	67.1
Costa Rica	10	7562	129,555	75.4	17.1	5679	75.1
Ecuador	11	6972	85,375	68.6	12.3	5841	83.8
Panama	12	4941	132,191	80.6	26.8	4262	86.3
Total and average		**1,058,093**	**11,092,647**	**71.1**	**13.3**	**418,614**	**61.5**

Source: ESI-InCites dataset updated 2017-04-15. Includes Web of Science content indexed through 2017-02-03.

Table 4.
Productivity ranking of Latin American countries in 2000–2016.

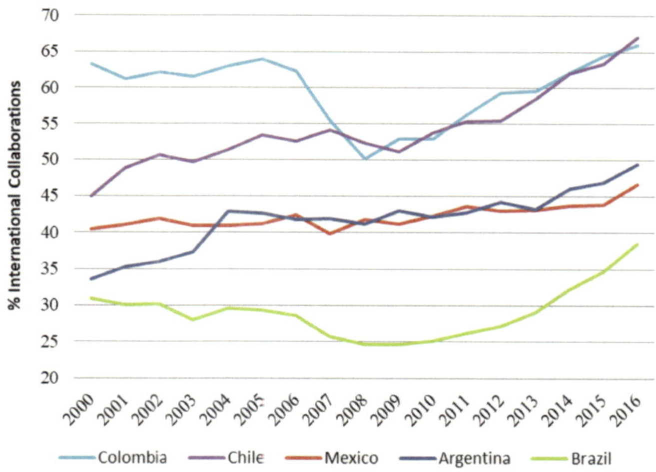

Figure 4.
International collaborations in scientific publications in Latin American countries in 2000–2016. Source: ESI-InCites dataset updated 2017-04-15. Includes Web of Science content indexed through 2017-02-03.

In the case of the BRICS countries, South Africa is the country with the highest international collaboration rate (48.0%) and the country with the highest impact (12.2) (**Table 2**). **Figure 5** illustrates the recent evolution (2000–2016) of the international collaboration of the BRICS countries. With the exception of South Africa that exploits international collaboration at a level similar to the more developed countries, the other members of the group have much lower rates. Brazil, which has had an oscillating collaboration rate since the beginning of the period, has resumed a stronger growth from 2010 onwards, surpassing in 2015 the index of international cooperation shown by Russia.

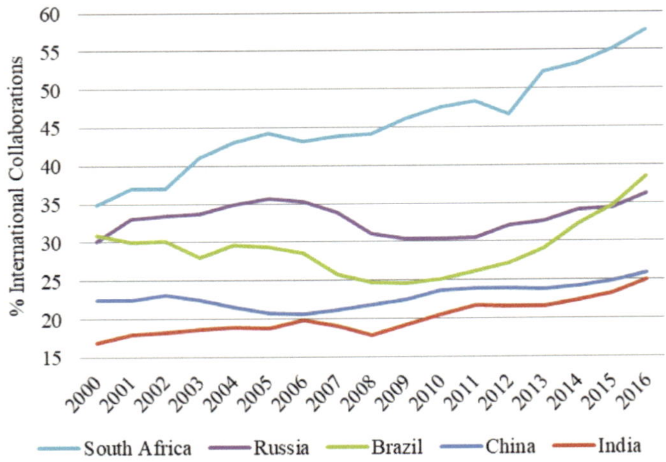

Figure 5.
International collaborations in scientific publications in WoS of the BRICS countries in 2000–2016. Source: ESI-InCites dataset updated 2017-04-15. Includes Web of Science content indexed through 2017-02-03.

Country		Total country articles	Collaboration with Brazil		Collaboration on data from Brazil %
			Total articles	Collaboration %	
Latin American					
1	Mexico	175,970	5495	3,1	1.0
2	Argentina	133,349	9404	7.1	1.7
3	Chile	87,419	5007	5.7	0.9
4	Colombia	42,021	4954	11.8	0.9
5	Venezuela	11,920	1722	14.5	0.3
6	Cuba	12,892	1692	13.1	0.3
7	Peru	14,331	1651	11.5	0.3
8	Uruguay	21,667	1251	5.8	0.2
9	Costa Rica	6972	1009	14.5	0.2
10	Ecuador	7562	664	8.8	0.1
11	Panama	4941	421	8.5	0.1
BRICS					
1	China	2,275,635	5818	0.3	1.1
2	Russia	713,637	5401	0.8	1.0
3	India	510,662	4742	0.9	0.9
4	South Africa	147,248	2737	1.9	0.5
Brazil		**539,049**	—	—	—

Source: ESI-InCites dataset updated 2017-04-15. Includes Web of Science content indexed through 2017-02-03.

Table 5.
Scientific collaborations of Latin American and BRICS countries with Brazil in 2000–2016.

Based on the set of results shown for the Latin American and BRICS countries, we analyzed the scientific cooperation of these countries with Brazil. **Table 5** shows the total production data of the Latin American countries and the components of the BRICS group, the number of joint publications with Brazil, and the respective percentage of collaboration of these countries with Brazil. The indices of collaboration in joint publications of Brazilian scientists with the Latin American or from BRICS countries are extremely low. Moreover, taking as an example the cooperation of the Latin American countries with Brazil shown in **Table 5**, it can be seen that the percentage of articles coming from this cooperation weighs much less on the total of Brazilian publications than on each of the partner countries, indicating that the rates of scientific cooperation among the countries of the region are very low when compared to the levels of international cooperation shown by these countries, as seen in **Table 5**. For Mexico's production, for example, this figure represents only 3.1% of its total scientific output and 14.5% for Costa Rica. For the estimation of this weight on Brazilian scientific production, the levels are even lower, varying from 0.1% (Panama and Costa Rica) to 1.7% with Argentina. A similar situation occurs when one compares the collaboration between scientists from BRICS countries and Brazil. That is, collaboration in the research projects of these countries, components of these two important trade blocs with Brazil, is practically nonexistent, suggesting that scientific and technological cooperation does not assume any significance in the context of these official partnerships. Nonetheless, such treaties emphasize that cooperation must include not only economic aspects but also scientific partnerships. Conversely, it has been observed for Latin American countries (data not shown) that intra-regional collaborations are much weaker than collaborations with developed countries. A similar situation was identified by Finardi [11] and Finardi and Buratti [12] for the BRICS case.

4. Brazilian situation in the analyzed context

In this article, special emphasis was given on the influence of international cooperation on the qualitative performance of scientific production. In the analysis presented here, which identifies in the low international scientific collaboration the unfavorable position of Brazil as concerned to the citations and impact of its publications, whether in the world context or in its position among the countries of the two economic blocs in which it participates, the MERCOSUL and BRICS. It is important, however, to point out that other factors, not discussed in this article, can influence the impact of scientific publications such as the size of the scientific community in each area of knowledge, the language, the maturity level of the areas in each country (or even the global world maturity of the same areas), and the degree of priority given by government agents to the technical and scientific development of certain areas with a view to explore comparative advantages as well as focusing the economic and social development of the countries.

As noted in an earlier study, the unbalanced and asymmetric international collaboration introduces profound distortions in the qualitative data of scientific production (citations, impact, world impact) of numerous countries and in the world, thus interfering in the expectations of scientific, technological, social, and economic development of the countries dependent on this type of international cooperation [14]. In this sense, in a recent article, Silva [22] deals with the relationship between productivity aspects and the quality of scientific production in the countries. The author makes severe criticism regarding comparisons of the scientific performance of Latin American countries. The author points out that it would not be appropriate to congratulate to some countries based on a simple analysis of these issues, since some countries have differentiated productivity in terms of their research and development priorities, with a high degree of self-financing, whereas the scientific production in other countries is highly dependent on the participation of international research groups and external financing. In our opinion, this observation is aligned with a high degree of international collaboration. It remains to be seen whether in such situations there are the expected technical and socioeconomic advances that this circumstance imposes on the dependent countries.

Concerning the specific case of Brazil, it is observed that the sharp growth of scientific production (see **Figure 1**) occurred in a short period of about four decades. This growth is clearly linked to the postgraduate programs since its installation in the late 1960s, resulting in the domestic training of thousands of teachers and doctors as well as research groups in universities and other centers, throughout the country. Although many researchers have enjoyed the possibility of partial or full training abroad since the 1970s, international collaboration in comparison with other countries has been less intensified and restricted to a few groups more oriented toward this form of production of new knowledge. This resulted in the small participation of Brazil in cooperative projects worldwide, a situation that affects, above all, the citations and, consequently, the impact of Brazilian science.

Nonetheless, it is also noted that, in several areas, the result of this domestic scientific development allowed Brazil to occupy a prominent position worldly wise. Examples are the work in the fields of tropical medicine, dentistry, parasitology, agriculture, energy, biofuels, and more recently, in the studies on Zika virus and microcephaly. Also, as a result of the recognized qualification of human resources through the postgraduate courses and the consolidation of research groups in strategic areas, many technological sectors have had great development in recent years. Examples are deep water oil exploration, tropical agriculture, pulp and paper industry, aircraft production, offshore platforms, the metal-mechanic working industry, alcohol and biofuels, and banking automation, among others. The results of this development can be seen in the fact that Brazil occupies outstanding economic position (ninth) [23] in the ranking of the countries with the highest GDP in the world wise and the second (after the USA) highest per capita GDP (US $ 15,359) among the most populous countries in the world.

Thus, the scientific and technological output of Brazil in several fields seems to confirm that the presence of internal training in human resources and infrastructure for research and development, even in the absence of strong international cooperation, can make it possible to attain significant scientific and socioeconomic advances in a short period of time. On the other hand, quantitatively unbalanced and technically asymmetric international cooperation, as is the case with about 70% of the countries analyzed recently [14], is certainly disastrous in enabling these countries to reach adequate levels of development to confront their social and economic challenges.

5. Conclusions

In this analysis, it can be observed that the impact of publications and, consequently, the greater visibility of science are directly influenced by the index of international collaboration between peers in the same area or related areas. This was evidenced in relation to the most productive countries and in the comparison of Brazil with Latin American countries and with the component countries of the BRICS group.

In the context of scientific production, international collaborations bring mutual benefits to partner countries, and in a broader and wider sense, they promote the social and economic prosperity of the groups involved. However, it should be noted that there should be an expected balance in these partnerships. As analyzed recently [14], the unbalanced and asymmetric scientific cooperation that occurs between many countries with very low scientific production but with a high impact due to the participation in the publications of articles coming from international cooperation with developed countries masks the importance of the contribution of S&T to help these country's development. This situation, above all, eludes the prospects of obtaining technological, economic, and social advances from the nations dependent on such cooperation, to face their own challenges such as in food production, the provision of drinking water, food and health security, energy supply, public safety, and environmental protection, all of which are typical global problems requiring a scientific approach to their solutions and generation of sustainable development perspectives.

Author details

Cristina Haeffner[1,2], Sonia Regina Zanotto[3], Helena B. Nader[4] and Jorge Almeida Guimarães[5]*

1 Post-graduate program in Science Education: Chemistry of Life and Health (PPGQVS) – Federal University of Rio Grande do Sul (UFRGS), Porto Alegre, Brazil

2 Faculty of Health Sciences Moinhos de Vento – Moinhos de Vento Hospital, Porto Alegre, Brazil

3 Brazilian Institute of Geography and Statistics (IBGE/RS), Porto Alegre, Brazil

4 Department of Biochemistry, Paulista Medical School, Federal University of São Paulo (UNIFESP), São Paulo, Brazil

5 Hospital of Clinics of Porto Alegre; Biotechnology Center – Federal University of Rio Grande do Sul (UFRGS), Porto Alegre, RS, Brazil

*Address all correspondence to: jguimaraes14@gmail.com

References

[1] Katz JS, Martin BR. What is research collaboration? Research Policy. 1997;**26**(1):1-18. DOI: 10.1016/S0048-7333(96)00917-1

[2] Wagner C, Park HW, Leydesdorff L. The continuing growth of global cooperation networks in research: A conundrum for national governments. PLoS One. 2015;**10**(7):e0131816. DOI: 10.1371/journal.pone.0131816

[3] Bouabid H, Paul-Hus A, Larivière V. Scientific collaboration and high-technology exchanges among BRICS and G-7 countries. Scientometrics. 2016;**106**(3):873-899. DOI: 10.1007/s11192-015-1806-0

[4] Sonnenwald DH. Scientific collaboration. Annual Review of Information Science and Technology. 2007;**41**(1):643-681. DOI: 10.1002/aris.2007.1440410121

[5] Leta J, Chaimovich H. Recognition and international collaboration: The Brazilian case. Scientometrics. 2002;**53**(3):325-335. DOI: 10.1023/A:1014868928349

[6] Glänzel W, Schubert A. Domesticity and internationality in co-authorship, references and citations. Scientometrics. 2005;**65**(3):323-342. DOI: 10.1007/s11192-005-0277-0

[7] Vanz SA. As redes atuais de colaboração científica no Brasil [thesis]. Porto Alegre: Universidade Federal do Rio Grande do Sul. Faculdade de Biblioteconomia e Comunicação - Programa de Pós-Graduação em Comunicação e Informação; 2009

[8] Vanz SA, Stumpf IRC. Colaboração científica: Revisão teórico conceitual. Perspectivas em Ciência da Informação. 2010;**15**(2):42-55

[9] Santin DM, Vanz SA, Stumpf IR. Collaboration networks in the Brazilian scientific output in evolutionary biology: 2000-2012. An. Acad. Brasil. Ciênc. 2016;**88**(1):165-178. DOI: 10.1590/0001-3765201620140620

[10] Guimaraes JA. The world of citations. A challenge for Latin American science. Interciencia -Caracas. 2000;**25**(4):182-185

[11] Finardi U. Scientific collaboration between BRICS countries. Scientometrics. 2015;**102**(2):1139-1166. DOI: 10.1007/s11192-014-1490-5

[12] Finardi U, Buratti A. Scientific collaboration framework of BRICS countries: An analysis of international co-authorship. Scientometrics. 2016;**109**(1):433-446. DOI: 10.1007/s11192-016-1927-0

[13] Pupo GA, Danta YR, Pupo YL. Correlación entre las medidas de centralidad de los países y el impacto de sus artículos. Caso de estudio de la investigación sobre biotecnología en Latinoamérica. Investigación bibliotecológica. 2016;**30**(69):75-94

[14] Zanotto SR, Haeffner C, Guimarães JA. Unbalanced international collaboration affects adversely the usefulness of countries' scientific output as well as their technological and social impact. Scientometrics. 2016;**109**(3):1789-1814. DOI: 10.1007/s11192-016-2126-8

[15] Guimarães JA, Humann MC. Training of human resources in science and technology in Brazil. The importance of a vigorous postgraduate program and its impact on the development of the Country. Scientometrics. 1995;**34**(1):101-119. DOI: 10.1007/BF02019176

[16] Bornmann L, Leydesdorff L. Macro-indicators of citation impacts of six prolific countries: InCites data and the

statistical significance of trends. PLoS One. 2013;**8**(2):e56768. DOI: 10.1371/journal.pone.0056768

[17] Guimarães JA. A pesquisa médica e biomédica no Brasil: Comparações com o desempenho científico brasileiro e mundial. Ciência & Saúde Coletiva. 2004;**9**(2):303-327

[18] Almeida ECE, Guimarães JA. Brazil's growing production of scientific articles—how are we doing with review articles and other qualitative indicators? Scientometrics. 2013;**97**(2):287-315. DOI: 10.1007/s11192-013-0967-y

[19] Cross D, Thomson S, Sinclair A. Research in Brazil: A report for CAPES by Clarivate Analytics [Internet]. 2017. Available from: https://www.capes.gov.br/images/stories/download/diversos/17012018-CAPES-InCitesReport-Final.pdf [Accessed: March 30, 2018]

[20] CNPq. Painel do Diretório dos grupos de pesquisa [Internet]. 2017. Available from: http://lattes.cnpq.br/web/dgp/painel-dgp [Accessed: May 11, 2017]

[21] Leydesdorff L, Bornmann L, Wagner CS. The relative influences of government funding and international collaboration on citation impact. Journal of the Association for Information Science and Technology. 2019;**70**(2):198-201

[22] Silva V. Scientometrics: Nature Index and Brazilian science. An. Acad. Brasil. Ciênc. 2016;**88**(3):1597-1599

[23] World Bank. World development indicators database. 2017. Available from: http://data.worldbank.org [Accessed: January 12, 2018]

Section 4

The Future of Scientometry

Chapter 6

Scientometrics as a Powerful Tool in Integrating Isolated Medical Specialties: A Case Study of the Rediscovery of the Luigi Cornaro Diet

Ligen Yu, Boxuan Yu and Bowei Yu

Abstract

Modern medicine is divided into different specialties. While well-trained experts can serve the patients better, each medical specialty is isolated to itself. For example, it is a norm for gastroenterology that fasting can lead to gastrointestinal tract (GIT) mucosa atrophy, and make the patient prone to bacterial translocation and sepsis. Yet, physiologists still think that fasting might be a feasible solution for obesity and related illnesses, as it can trigger autophagy which has multiple physiological functions benefiting the body. In this chapter, using the rediscovery of the Luigi Cornaro diet as an example, we demonstrate that scientometrics methods can be a powerful tool to integrate the isolated medical specialties. The Luigi Cornaro diet is able to maintain the homeostasis of GIT mucosa while keeping a serum starvation to fit for a rare physiological condition of fully developed sustained upregulated autophagy (SUA) in the body. Although fully developed SUA is relatively rare, low-grade upregulated autophagy (UA) is quite common, reflected by the prevalence of obesity in population. UA is the main component of our self-healing capacity, and the connector between infection and obesity. Such discovery of scientometrics could be the next generation medical practice.

Keywords: Bibliometrics analysis, medical specialties, isolation, integration, Luigi Cornaro diet, upregulated autophagy, sustained upregulated autophagy, self-healing

1. Introduction

Just as the division of labor in every single field of activity is an emblematic feature of modern society, medical specialization is now a self-evident necessity in medical science and medical practice [1]. Nowadays we are not expecting any general practitioner to address life-threatening diseases of specific organs in the body, as highly specialized medical specialists are more professional and productive, as they make better diagnoses, fewer mistakes than general internists and general practitioners do [2]. Medical science research follows the same trend, and the importance of specialization in medical science should not be slighted.

While Hippocrates (and basically every one after him) described disease as occurring when there is an imbalance between the four 'humors' (phlegm, black bile, yellow bile and blood) [3], today's medical specialists know any of the human organ and any disease in more detail than the physicians in the time of Hippocrates did.

Yet, the specialization of medical research creates a vast amount of medical knowledge, which is also expanding exponentially in such a way that no medical specialist can grasp this medical knowledge in all [4–10]. As a result, specialists are more or less focused on their own specialties, and isolated from other specialties. For example, it is a norm for gastroenterology that fasting can lead to gastrointestinal tract (GIT) mucosa atrophy, causing the patient to be prone to bacterial translocation and sepsis [11–13]. Yet, physiologists still think that fasting might be a feasible solution for obesity and related illness, as it can trigger autophagy which has multiple physiological functions benefiting to the body [14, 15].

This problem might not be solved by the specialists themselves, simply because it takes a lot of time for them to become specialists, and they may not have the time to spare on other specialties. Here comes the scientometrics, we are not specialists on any medical division, so we may not have detailed knowledge on any of the medical divisions. Yet, we specialize in literature analysis. By analyzing the connections among the literatures from various specialties of medical researches, we may break the isolation, find the close relations among them, and integrate them.

Here we give the rediscovery of Luigi Cornaro diet as a case study.

Luigi Cornaro (1464–1566) was a Venetian noble man. He lived freely when he was young before 35 or 40. After a severe illness at the age around 40, he began to reduce his diet under medical advice. At the age of 70–80, he restricted himself to a daily allowance of 12 ounces of solid food and 14 ounces of new wine. Later in his life, he found that he could support his life and strength with no more food than the yolk of an egg with a few spoonful milk with bread in the 24 hours. He was so habituated to this simple diet that when he was about 70 years of age the addition of 2 ounces a day had proved fatal. His diet was so effective in keeping him in good health that his strength and all his senses were kept in very good condition throughout his lifetime. His book, The Art of Living Long [16], is one of the most successful diet books, which is still in print over 460 years after it was first published in Padua in 1558. It was an instant success, went through many editions, and was translated into many languages.

Despite the success of Luigi Cornaro's own practice and his books, common people find that his diet is very difficult to follow. This even happened at the time of Luigi Cornaro. In his discourses [16], he had repeatedly mentioned that it was extremely hard for ordinary people to follow his diet. For example, he said: "Now, I am often at a loss to understand why men of fine parts and understanding, who have attained middle age, do not, when they find themselves attacked by disorders and sickness, betake themselves to a regular life, and that constantly."; "One of the younger of them said that I appeared to enjoy the special grace of being able to relinquish, with ease, one kind of life, and embrace another, a thing which he knew from theory to be feasible, but in practice to be difficult, for it had proved as hard to him, as easy to me."; "There are some sensualists, my Lord, who say that I have thrown away my time and trouble, in writing a treatise upon temperance, and other discourses on the same subject; alleging, that it is impossible to conform to it."

In the nineteenth century, German philosopher Friedrich Nietzsche read Luigi Cornaro's book, tried the diet and commented that Luigi Cornaro was "mistaking the consequence for the cause" [17]. Nietzsche said: "The worthy Italian saw in his diet the cause of his long life: while the prerequisite of long life, an extraordinarily slow metabolism, a small consumption, was the cause of his meagre diet. He was not free to eat much or little as he chose, his frugality was not an act of 'free will': he became ill when he ate more."

Although the Luigi Cornaro diet is very hard to follow by ordinary people, it is not impossible. There are people who are actually following this diet without their self-awareness. In our contemporary days, Prime Minister of Malaysia Tun Dr. Mahathir bin Mohamad is an example. According to a report of The Strait Times [18], Dr. Mahathir has a slice of bread for breakfast, has whatever the cook at home prepares for lunch, and has two spoonful of rice at night. This food amount may actually be less than the 12 ounces of solid food a day of Luigi Cornaro. Dr. Mahathir's diet may explain why at his current age of 93, he is still vigorous, and all his senses are as good as middle-aged persons, which is exactly the situation described by Luigi Cornaro [16].

Because of the practical importance of the Luigi Cornaro diet, we are interested in the biological process behind the diet. This biological process should be able to answer the following two questions:

1. How is the balance of energy and nutrition maintained in the body with such a low food intake in this diet?

2. How can this biological process effectively defend against common diseases like infection and the degeneration of body cells so that one's strength and senses are not as affected while one is aging?

In this chapter we will describe how we apply the Bibliometrics analysis method to the publications on topics relating to the Luigi Cornaro diet, and find that a rare physiological condition of fully developed sustained upregulated autophagy (SUA) is the answer to the above two questions [19]. This finding also explains why the Luigi Cornaro diet is not fit for ordinary people who can eat normally.

2. Literature survey on Luigi Cornaro diet and interpretation

Luigi Cornaro and his diet are mentioned in most of the dieting books. Nevertheless, modern medicine has very scarce literature on Luigi Cornaro. When we search "Luigi Cornaro" as keyword in Web of Science, only four papers can be found. Three of them were published in 1901 in Lancet, and one paper published in 2018 by Journal of The History of Medicine and Allied Sciences. These papers are not able to provide any useful medical explanations to the Luigi Cornaro diet.

In the discourses of Luigi Cornaro, he wrote [16]: "When men are taken ill they discontinue, or nearly so, their food. ... by reducing themselves to a small quantity, they recover from the jaws of death." What Cornaro described here is illness induced anorexia (IIA), and he employed IIA to justify his diet. So we turn to publications on anorexia (loss of appetite as a physiological symptom), especially search for publications on illness (infection, sickness) induced anorexia (IIA) as the start of our analysis.

2.1 Illness induced anorexia (IIA) accompanying upregulated autophagy (UA)

Decreased food consumption (anorexia) is the most common sign of infection and severe injury [20]. It is believed that IIA is an active host defense strategy for pathogen elimination and enhancing healing of injury [21–23]. Unlike the starvation-invoked regulatory mechanisms aim at conservation of protein mass in healthy subjects, patients with illness induced anorexia have increased energy expenditure and protein catabolism, associated with profound neuroendocrine alterations [23].

In Web of Science, we can find 53 papers on illness induced anorexia. **Figure 1** shows the mapping of terms used in the titles and abstracts in these 53 papers using the VOSViewer Bibliometrics analysis software, which is developed by CWTS of Leiden University. Two papers relating illness induced anorexia to upregulation of autophagy catch our attention [24, 25], as highlighted in **Figure 1**.

Autophagy is the degradation of intracellular components in lysosomes to remove altered or dysfunctional proteins and organelles [26, 27]. It is a highly regulated process in eukaryotes to maintain homeostasis and manage stress responses. It has multiple physiological functions including cellular quality control, energetic

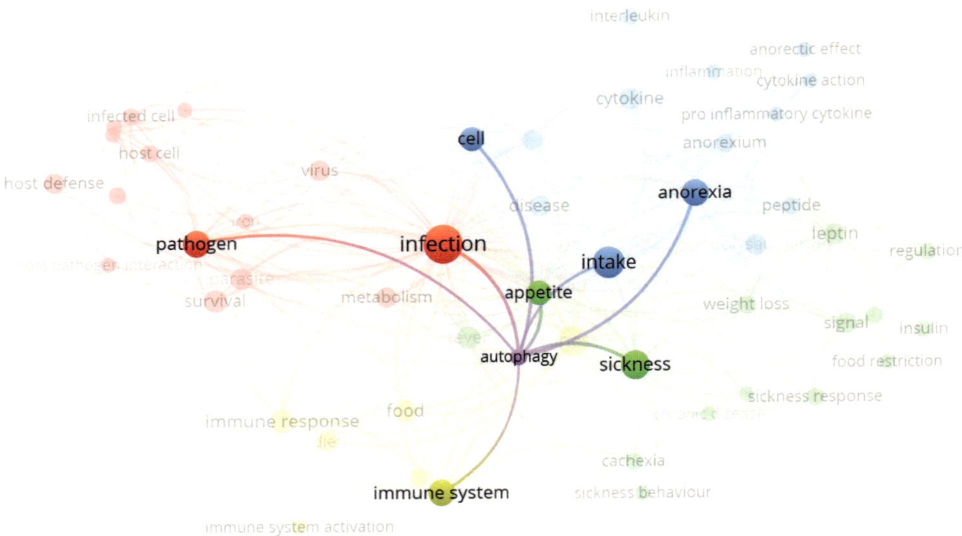

Figure 1.
Illness-induced anorexia is related to autophagy.

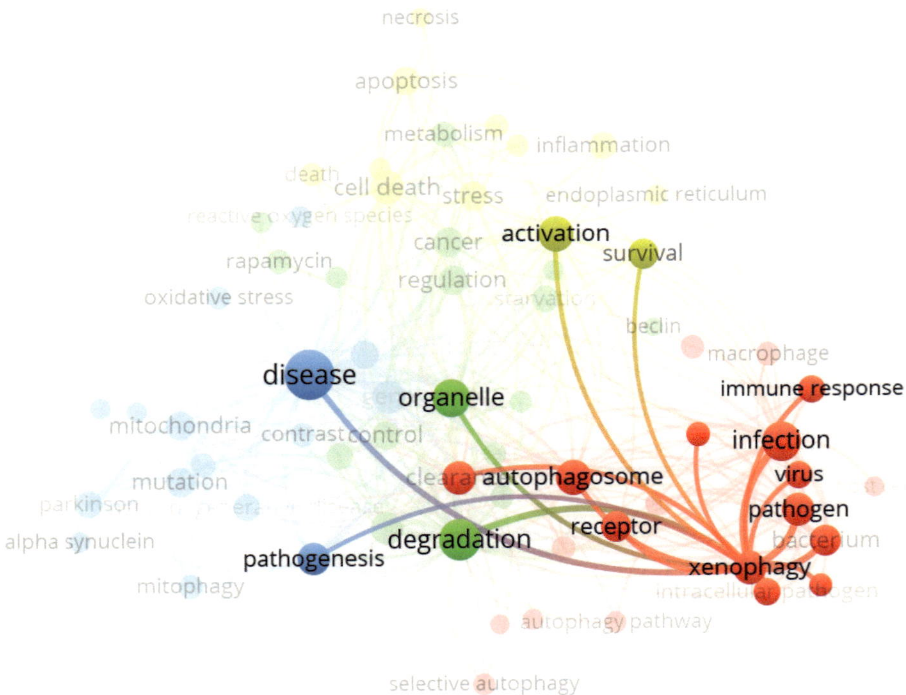

Figure 2.
Autophagy (xenophagy) is closely related to infection (pathogen) elimination.

balance maintenance, and pathogen cleaning [28]. In normal physiological conditions, a low level of basal or constitutive autophagy occurs to maintain cellular homeostasis by controlling the turnover of damaged proteins and organelles [29]. In pathological conditions (like infection or injury), autophagy as an adaptive cellular mechanism will be upregulated to eliminate pathogens and recycle and reutilize damaged macromolecules and organelles [26, 27]. During an infection, upregulated autophagy has a specific role in the capture and degradation of intracellular bacteria and viruses to reinstall health, a process termed as xenophagy [30–32].

In Web of Science, we can find more than 19,000 publications relating illness (infection, sickness, and disease) to autophagy, showing the close relation of autophagy to infectious pathogen elimination. The term analysis of the top 700 highly cited papers of these 19,000 papers is shown in **Figure 2**, with the keyword "xenophagy" highlighted.

Xenophagy as a catabolic process is able to recycle and reutilize the degraded pathogen components for energy or protein synthesis, it provides the host with plenty of energy and nutrients during the process. So our interpretation of IIA is that, in order to avoid over-nutrition, our body intentionally induced anorexia (loss of appetite) as a counter measure against upregulated autophagy.

2.2 Upregulated autophagy (UA) as the connector between infection and obesity

It has been noticed that infection can enhance one's proneness to develop obesity, and the term infectobesity was coined by Dr. Nikhil V. Dhurandhar in 2001 [33]. Yet the connection between infection and obesity is unclear. Given the close relation of autophagy to infection elimination, we searched publications on infection induced obesity together with autophagy, and 238 publications are found in Web of Science. **Figure 3** shows the terms used in titles and abstracts of these publications, and autophagy is an obvious connector for infection and obesity.

Based on **Figure 3**, we suspect that, chronic low-grade inflammation triggered low-grade upregulated autophagy (UA), yet the inflammation degree is so low that the inflammation is not accompanied by fever and illness-induced anorexia. This low-grade upregulated autophagy provides certain amount of recycled energy and nutrients to the body of the host. Over nutrition and excessive energy will occur if one still eats normally. These energy and nutrients accumulate inside the body over the years, and lead to obesity. Therefore, obesity is a good indicator of low grade UA. As the degree of obesity is related to the degree of UA, and UA is generally protective, it should not be alerted if a person is slightly overweight or obese without accompanying with metabolic diseases like high blood pressure, diabetes, cardiovascular disease. Also, as the degree of UA grows with aging, older people can generally be healthier than young people, if old people can lower their food intake according to the degree of their UA when they are growing older.

2.3 Sustained upregulated autophagy (SUA) and the Luigi Cornaro diet

The biological process of triggering upregulated autophagy with or without the accompanying illness induce anorexia by infection/inflammation cannot explain the Luigi Cornaro diet, as Luigi Cornaro never fell ill after he adopted his simple diet. So we take a step further to hypothesize that Luigi Cornaro had a rare condition of fully developed sustained upregulated autophagy (SUA) without anorexia (loss of appetite) [19]. And we have provided the possible cause and the feature of SUA in our paper [19]. As SUA is able to provide plenty of recycled energy and nutrients to the body from each cell in the body, regular restrictive eating is now compulsory. The small amount of food is mainly used to maintain the homeostasis of the GIT mucosa [19]. Thus, we answer the question set out by Dr. Ernest Van

Someren in 1901 [34]: "Did he (Luigi Cornaro) make use of a physiological process unknown to us, of the value of which he was not cognisant?" This also explain why the Luigi Cornaro diet cannot be adopted by ordinary people.

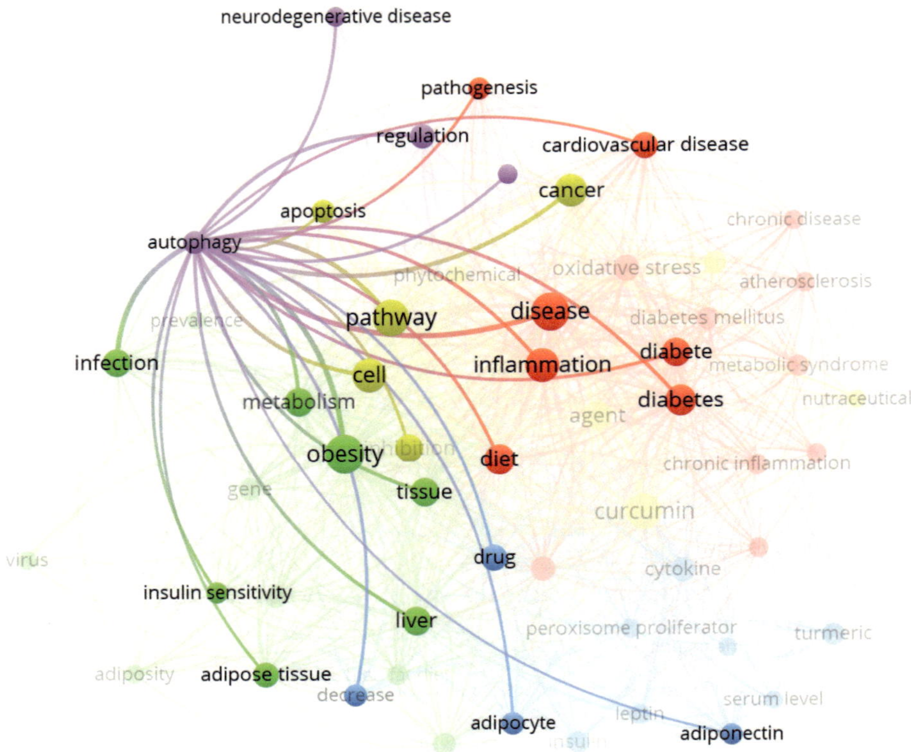

Figure 3.
The close relations among infection, autophagy and obesity.

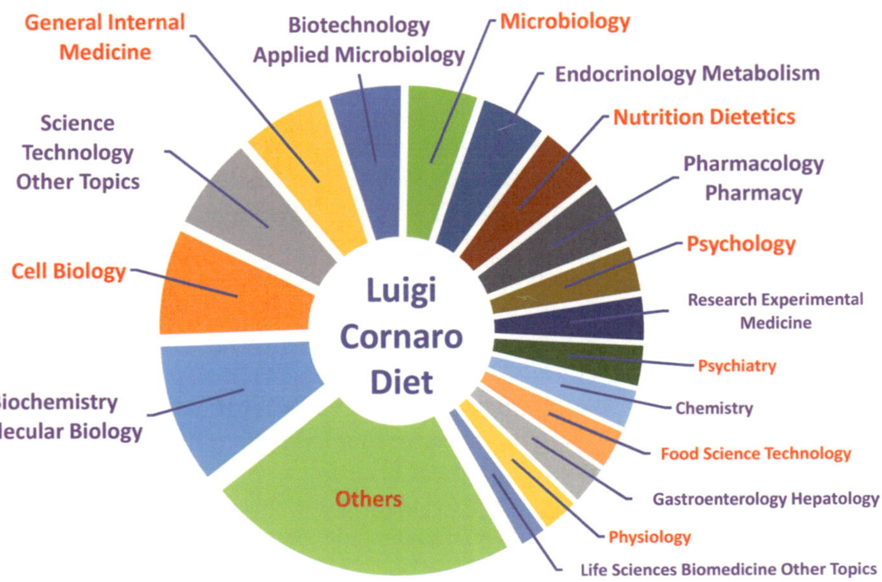

Figure 4.
Research areas of publications used to interpret Luigi Cornaro diet.

2.4 The interpretation of Luigi Cornaro diet requires knowledge from multiple medical disciplines

In the Bibliometrics analysis on Luigi Cornaro diet above, we have searched publications in different research areas of medical science, as shown in **Figure 4**. The extensive research on autophagy in the last 60 years helps us in understanding the biological process behind the simple Luigi Cornaro diet of Eat-but-Little. Autophagy itself is a multidisciplinary research topic. And the understanding of Luigi Cornaro diet also requires knowledge from gastroenterology, infectious diseases, food science and technology, psychology and so on.

3. The possible therapeutic application of the Luigi Cornaro diet

3.1 Research on the self-healing capacity of human being should be enhanced

The Luigi Cornaro diet clearly shows that our body has the self-healing capacity, with UA/SUA as its main component. We searched the term "self-healing" in Web of Science from 1990 to 2018, and 10,483 publications can be found. The Web of Science subject category analysis shows that most of the top 25 subject categories are in materials science and computer science, as shown in **Figure 5**. Only one subject category, dermatology, in the top 25 subject categories is related to medical science. Keyword analysis was carried out for these publications using VOSViewer, and 27,337 keywords are identified. Among these keywords, 2540 keywords have occurrences of five times and above, as shown in **Figure 6**. Using the clustering of keywords in the VOSViewer mapping in **Figure 6**, 11 topics are identified. **Table 1** gives the representative keywords in these 11 topics. It is very clear that, most of the keywords are on materials science and artificial intelligence of computer science. Furthermore, topic analysis on the keywords shows that the relative volume of self-healing research in medical science is shrinking in the last 29 years, from around 40% of the total publication in 1990 on self-healing to less than 10% in 2018, as shown in **Figure 7**. This is quite unusual, as "self-healing" is initially a medical term borrowed by materials science and computer science. So we suggest that the medical community should pay more attention to this self-healing capacity of the organs in our body, which can greatly lower the medical burden of every country in the world, and make our society more healthy.

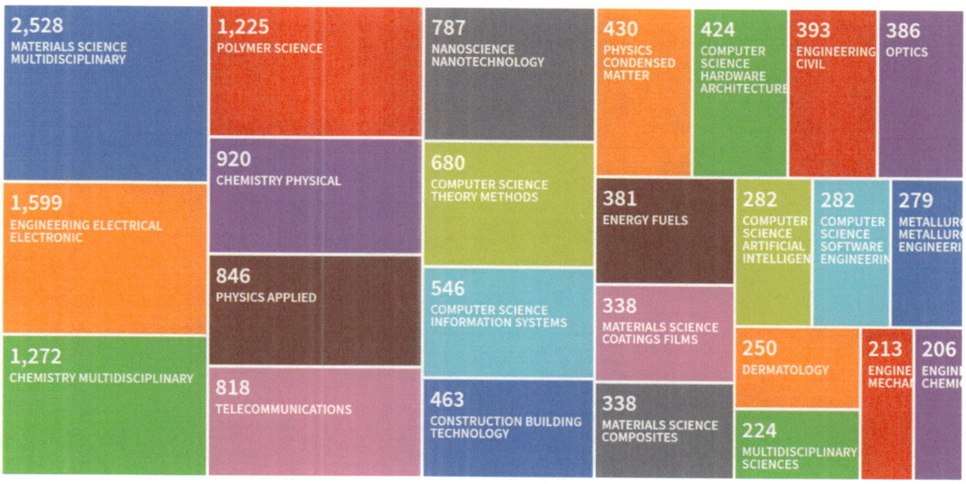

Figure 5.
Top 25 Web of Science subject categories for publication on "self-healing" during 1990–2018.

3.2 More caution should be placed on the use of total parenteral nutrition (TPN)

Parenteral nutrition (PN) is the administering of specialist nutritional products to a person by way of a vein, bypassing the usual process of eating and digestion (referred as enteral nutrition). Total parenteral nutrition (TPN) was introduced by Dudrick et al. in clinical practice over 50 years ago [35]. The principal indication for TPN is a seriously ill patient where enteral feeding is not possible.

For critically ill patients, there is an ongoing debate on whether providing them with early enteral nutrition, or tolerating permissive underfeeding. Recently ESICM clinical practice guidelines [36] and the Surviving Sepsis Campaign [37] all suggest using early enteral nutrition (EEN), initiated at a low rate, in the majority of critically ill patients, and suggest delaying EN only in some special cases like in patients with uncontrolled shock, uncontrolled hypoxemia and acidosis, and other sever complications. These suggestions agrees well with our finding about the Luigi

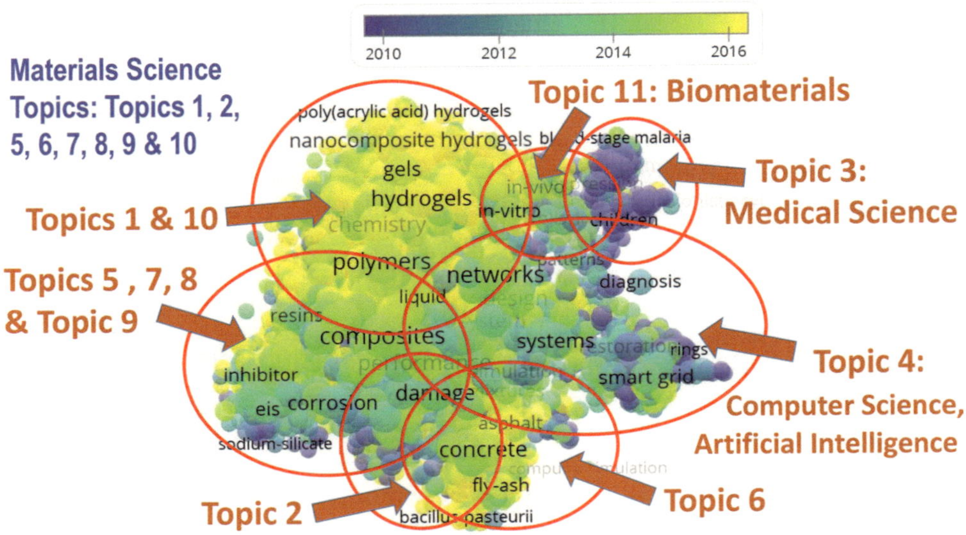

Figure 6.
Most of the publications on self-healing are in materials science and artificial intelligence.

T1: Polymer	T2: Ceramic Coatings	T3: Medical Science	T4: Computer Science and AI	T5: Thin Films	T6: Concrete
polymers	behavior	degradation	design	films	concrete
networks	temperature	cells	systems	corrosion protection	strength
hydrogels	oxidation	skin	model	corrosion	permeability
mechanical-properties	surface	self-healing reticulo-histiocytosis	smart grid	resistance	cracks
chemistry	microstructure	tissue	self healing	release	bacteria
T7: Composites	**T8: Nanocomposites**	**T9: Nanostructured membranes**	**T10: Dye-Doped Polymer**	**T11: Biomaterial**	-
composites	performance	coatings	polymer	drug-delivery	-
microcapsules	nanocomposites	nanoparticles	photodegradation	hydrogel	-
damage	carbon nanotubes	water	dye	in-vitro	-
repair	graphene	fabrication	stabilization	delivery	-
composite	graphene oxide	surfaces	biopolymer	chitosan	-

Table 1.
Representative keywords for topics on self-healing.

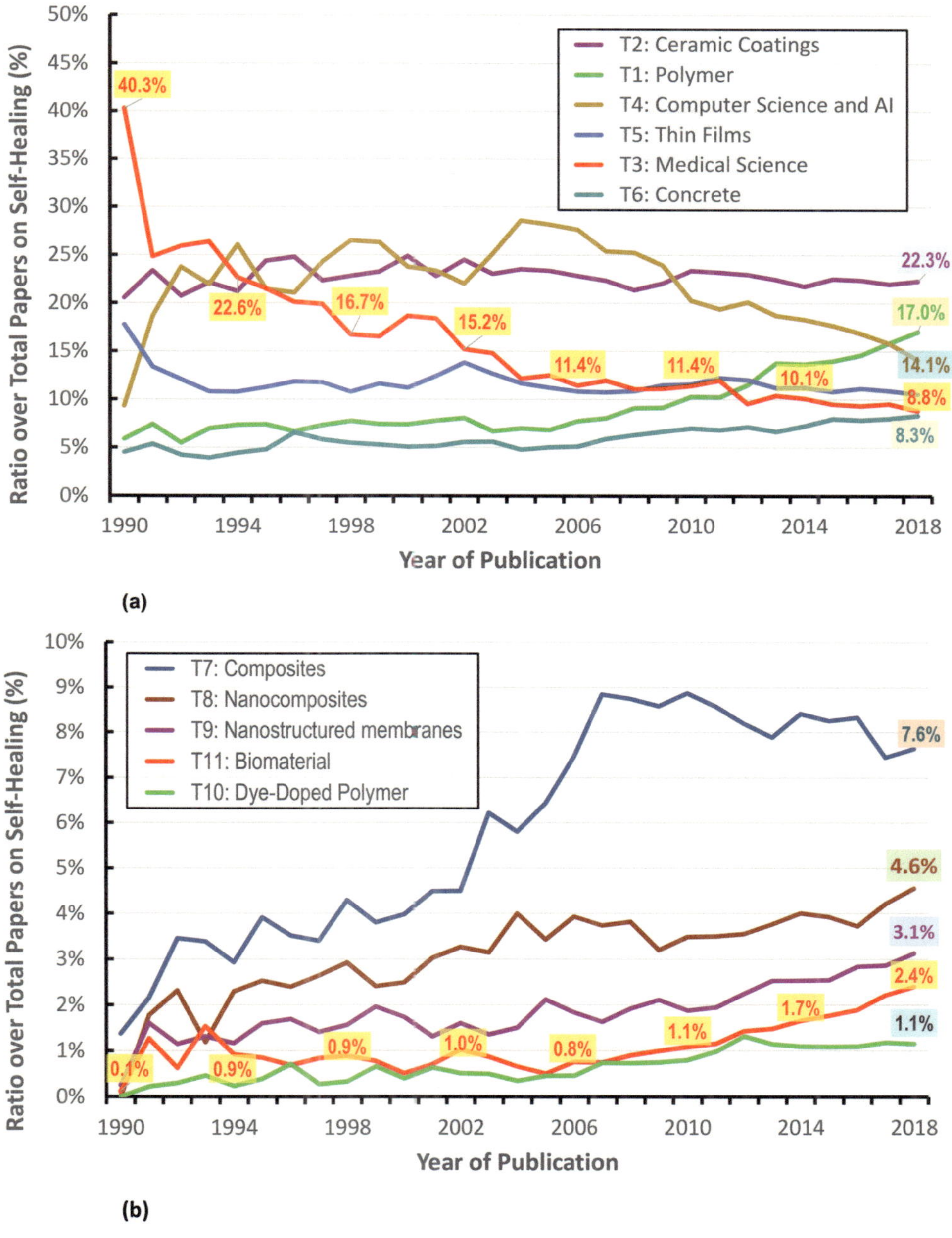

Figure 7.
(a) Relative volume trends of publications on topic 1 to topic 6 of self-healing. (b) Relative volume trends of publications on topic 7 to topic 11 of self-healing

Cornaro diet, since low rate early nutrition supports and protects the proper function of GIT mucosa, while the serum starvation ensures the full function of UA in the body, helping the patient in recovering from the illness by his own self-healing capacity.

While Luigi Cornaro diet introduce small amount of food in the GIT and keep a serum starvation to meet the requirement of SUA, TPN just does the opposite. It introduces nutrition to the blood to interfere the proper functioning of UA, depriving the body of a key cell survival mechanism. Furthermore, TPN starves the GIT, which may result in GIT mucosa atrophy and dysfunction. Research shows that it is critical to have small amount food in the GIT to maintain a full functioning GIT mucosa,

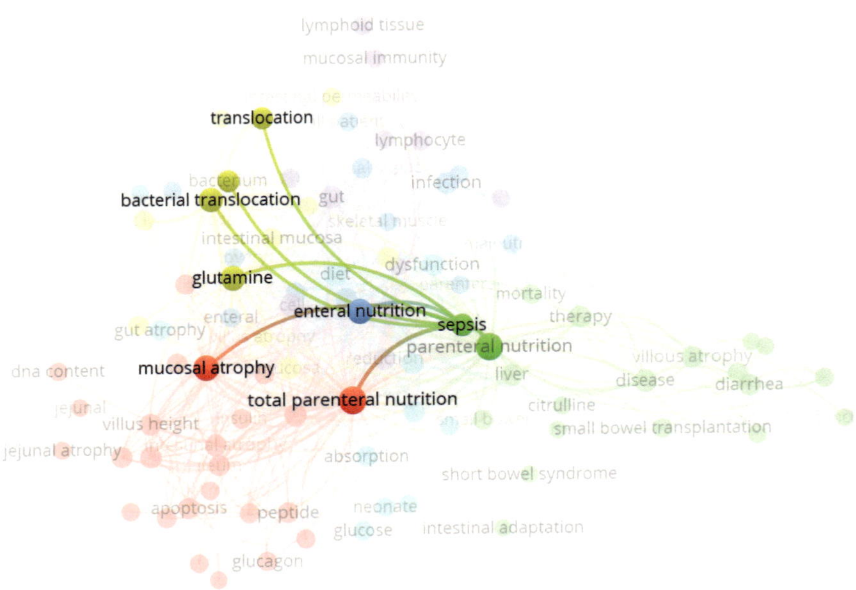

Figure 8.
Keywords analysis for publications on TPN shows the close relation of TPN to bacterial translocation and sepsis.

preventing it from atrophy, avoiding its proneness for bacterial translocation and sepsis [13]. **Figure 8** shows the keywords mapping of publications on TPN, with the term "sepsis" highlighted. We can clearly see the close relation of TPN to sepsis.

Based on the above discussion, we suggest that great caution should be placed on the use of TPN in treating sickness. TPN should only be conducted for seriously ill patients who are too emaciated to have proper running of SUA activity in their body, and enteral feeding is truly not possible.

4. Summary

Specialization is an established part of the medical landscape nowadays, and the importance of specialization in medical research and practice should not be disdained. Yet, specialists are more or less focused on their own specialties, and isolated from other specialties. Here we use the rediscovery of the Luigi Cornaro diet as an example to show that, scientometrics can be a powerful tool in integrating various isolated medical specialties. After its publication in 1558, the simple diet of Luigi Cornaro, "Eat but Little," puzzled people for over 460 years. By analyzing the keywords in the titles and abstracts of publications on topics related to the Luigi Cornaro diet, we find that the fully developed sustained upregulated autophagy (SUA) without anorexia is a pre-requisite for the Luigi Cornaro diet. The fully developed SUA performed a multifaceted role in helping Luigi Cornaro maintaining the energy and nutrition balance; and effectively defending the common diseases like infection and the degeneration of body cells. This was why he could keep health until the end of his days, and his strength and senses were not affected while he was aging. Considering the connections among infection, illness-induced anorexia, upregulated autophagy (UA) and obesity, and sustained upregulated autophagy (SUA) and the Luigi Cornaro diet uncovered by scientometric analysis coupled with a long history of anecdotal evidence, a carefully designed study should be undertaken to confirm the causal link and define the conditions under which a Cornaro diet should be medically advised.

5. Disclaimer

This chapter is based on the authors' limited personal experience and literature Surveys. The authors are not medical doctors and do not want to make medical recommendations. Instead, this chapter should be regarded as a thought-provoking impulse for future research. Neither the authors, the publisher, nor any other party who has been involved in the preparation or publication of this chapter guarantees that the information contained herein is in every respect accurate or complete. Therefore, this chapter is intended as reference only, and does not serve as a medical advice. The information in this publication is only to help you make informed decisions about your health. It is not intended as a substitute for any treatment that may have been prescribed by your doctor, who is familiar with your specific needs. If you suspect that you have a medical problem, we urge you to seek competent medical care.

Acknowledgements

The authors are greatly indebted to Dr. Bryan C. Hendrix from Advanced Deposition Materials, Entegris, USA for his valuable suggestions and English language checking.

Conflict of interest

On behalf of all authors, the corresponding author states that there is no conflict of interest.

Author details

Ligen Yu[1]*, Boxuan Yu[2] and Bowei Yu[3]

1 Talent Recruitment and Career Support (TRACS) Office, Nanyang Technological University, Singapore, Singapore

2 Hwa Chong Institution, Singapore, Singapore

3 School of Computing, National University of Singapore, Singapore, Singapore

*Address all correspondence to: mlgyu@ntu.edu.sg

References

[1] Weisz G. Divide and Conquer: A Comparative History of Medical Specialization. Oxford: Oxford University Press, 2005. 359 pp. (ISBN-10: 0-19-517969-2, ISBN-13: 978-0-19-517969-9)

[2] Mulligan CB. Reaping the Gains from Specialization. The New York Times [Internet]. 2009. Available from: https://economix.blogs.nytimes.com/2009/03/18/reaping-the-gains-from-specialization/ [Accessed: 15 February 2019]

[3] Yapijakis C. Hippocrates of Kos, the father of clinical medicine, and Asclepiades of Bithynia, the father of molecular medicine. In Vivo. 2009;**23**(4):507-514

[4] Densen P. Challenges and opportunities facing medical education. Transactions of the American Clinical and Climatological Association. 2011;**122**:48-58

[5] Alper BS, Hand JA, Elliott SG, Kinkade S, Hauan MJ, Onion DK, et al. How much effort is needed to keep up with the literature relevant for primary care? Journal of the Medical Library Association. 2004;**92**:429-437

[6] Druss BG, Marcus SC. Growth and decentralization of the medical literature: Implications for evidence-based medicine. Journal of the Medical Library Association. 2005;**93**:499-501

[7] Lee CH, Yoon HJ. Medical big data: Promise and challenges. Kidney Research and Clinical Practice. 2017;**36**:3-11. DOI: 10.23876/j.krcp.2017.36.1.3

[8] Casadevall A, Fang FC. Specialized science. Infection and Immunity. 2014;**82**:1355-1360. DOI: 10.1128/IAI.01530-13

[9] Weisz G. The emergence of medical specialization in the nineteenth century. Bulletin of the History of Medicine. 2003;**77**:536-575. DOI: 10.1353/bhm.2003.0150

[10] Emery N. Our Unsustainable Culture of Medical Specialization. The Atlantic [Internet]. 31 July 2012. Available from: https://www.theatlantic.com/health/archive/2012/07/our-unsustainableculture-of-medical-specialization/260504/ [Accessed: 15 February 2019]

[11] Zhou QQ, Yang DZ, Luo YJ, Li SZ, Liu FY, Wang GS. Over-starvation aggravates intestinal injury and promotes bacterial and endotoxin translocation under high-altitude hypoxic environment. World Journal of Gastroenterology. 2011;**17**:1584-1593. DOI: 10.3748/wjg.v17.i12.1584

[12] Funes SC, Filippa VP, Cid FD, Mohamed F, Caviedes-Vidal E, Chediack JG. Effect of fasting in the digestive system: Histological study of the small intestine in house sparrows. Tissue & Cell. 2014;**46**:356-362. DOI: 10.1016/j.tice.2014.406.007

[13] Shaw D, Gohil K, Basson MD. Intestinal mucosal atrophy and adaptation. World Journal of Gastroenterology. 2012;**18**(44):6357-6375. DOI: 10.3748/wjg.v18.i44.6357

[14] Longo VD, Mattson MP. Fasting: Molecular mechanisms and clinical applications. Cell Metabolism. 2014;**19**:181-192. DOI: 10.1016/j.cmet.2013.12.008

[15] Mattson MP, Longo VD, Harvie M. Impact of intermittent fasting on health and disease processes. Ageing Research Reviews. 2017;**39**:46-58. DOI: 10.1016/j.arr.2016.10.005

[16] Luigi Cornaro Online Writings on the Temperate Life [Internet].

Available from: http://soilandhealth.org/wp-content/uploads/02/0201hygli bcat/020105cornaro.html [Accessed: 15 February 2019]

[17] Nietzsche, Friedrich: Twilight of the Idols/the Anti-Christ. Translated by R.J. Hollingdale. London: Penguin books; 2003 p. 58. ISBN 0-140-44514-5

[18] The Strait Times. Lunch with Sumiko: Mahathir Mohamad's Unfinished Business as Malaysia Gears up for Election. Available from: https://www.straitstimes.com/asia/se-asia/mahathirs-unfinished-business [Accessed: 25 March 2018]

[19] Yu BX, Yu BW, Yu LG. Sustained upregulated autophagy (SUA) without anorexia—Aetiology of morbid obesity and anorexia nervosa. Journal of Obesity & Eating Disorders. 2019;**5**:1. DOI: 10.21767/2471-8203.100041

[20] Chang HR, Bistrian B. The role of cytokines in the catabolic consequences of infection and injury. Journal of Parenteral and Enteral Nutrition. 1998;**22**:156-166

[21] Exton MS. Infection-induced anorexia: Active host defence strategy. Appetite. 1997;**29**:369-383. DOI: 10.1006/appe.1997.0116

[22] Nilsson A. Mechanisms behind illness-induced anorexia [thesis]. Linköping University Medical Dissertations; No. 1549. 2016. Available from: https://liu.diva-portal.org/smash/get/diva2:1047669/FULLTEXT01.pdf

[23] Romijn JA. Substrate metabolism in the metabolic response to injury. The Proceedings of the Nutrition Society. 2000;**59**:447-449. DOI: 10.1017/S0029665100000616

[24] van Niekerk G, Loos B, Nell T, Engelbrecht AM. Autophagy—A free meal in sickness-associated anorexia. Autophagy. 2016;**12**(4):727-734. DOI: 10.1080/15548627.2016.1147672

[25] van Niekerk G, Isaacs AW, Nell T, Engelbrecht AM. Sickness-associated anorexia: Mother nature's idea of immunonutrition? Mediators of Inflammation. 2016;**2016**:8071539. DOI: 10.1155/2016/8071539

[26] Zhi XY, Feng WZ, Rong YG, Liu R. Anatomy of autophagy: From the beginning to the end. Cellular and Molecular Life Sciences. 2018;**75**(5): 815-831. DOI: 10.1007/s00018-017-2657-z

[27] Eskelinen EL, Saftig P. Autophagy: A lysosomal degradation pathway with a central role in health and disease. Biochimica et Biophysica Acta-Molecular Cell Research. 2009;**1793**:664-673. DOI: 10.1016/j.bbamcr.2008.07.014

[28] Sridhar S, Botbol Y, Macian F, Cuervo AM. Autophagy and disease: Always two sides to a problem. The Journal of Pathology. 2012;**226**:255-273. DOI: 10.1002/path.3025

[29] Levine B, Kroemer G. Autophagy in the pathogenesis of disease. Cell. 2008;**132**:27-42. DOI: 10.1016/j.cell.2007.12.018

[30] Kuballa P, Nolte WM, Castoreno AB, Xavier RJ. Autophagy and the immune system. Annual Review of Immunology. 2012;**30**:611. DOI: 10.1146/annurev-immunol-020711-074948

[31] Jo EK, Yuk JM, Shin DM, Sasakawa C. Roles of autophagy in elimination of intracellular bacterial pathogens. Frontiers in Immunology. 2013;**4**:UNSP 97. DOI: 10.3389/fimmu.2013.00097

[32] Gomes LC, Dikic I. Autophagy in antimicrobial immunity. Molecular Cell. 2014;**54**(2):224-233. DOI: 10.1016/j.molcel.2014.03.009

[33] Dhurandhar NV. Infectobesity: Obesity of infectious origin. Journal of Nutrition.

2001;**131**(10):2794S-2797S. DOI: 10.1093/jn/131.10.2794S

[34] Van Someren EH. Was Luigi Cornaro right? The British Medical Journal. 1901;**2**(2128):1082-1084. Available from: https://www.jstor.org/stable/20269899

[35] Dudrick SJ, Wilmore DW. Long terra parenteral nutrition with growth, development, and positive nitrogen balance. Surgery. 1968;**64**:134-142

[36] Reintam Blaser A, Starkopf J, Alhazzani W, et al. Early enteral nutrition in critically ill patients: ESICM clinical practice guidelines. Intensive Care Medicine. 2017;**43**:380-398. DOI: 10.1007/s00134-016-4665-0

[37] Rhodes A, Evans LE, Alhazzani W, et al. Surviving sepsis campaign: International guidelines for management of sepsis and septic shock: 2016. Intensive Care Medicine. 2017;**43**(3):304-377. DOI: 10.1007/s00134-017-4683-6